I dedicate this book to my Mother and
and understanding when I was a growir
wish to also dedicate the book to my fri(
recently discovered passed away just pri͡͞. .͞. .͞.͞ .͞.͞.͞.͞ . ͞.͞.͞.͞.͞.͞.͞ .͞.͞
write this book.

Front Cover Photo: 52322 & 2890 at Ramsbottom station on the East Lancs Railway on the 4th March 2018.

Back Cover Photo: 45562 (45699) on the Scarborough Spa Express arriving at York station on 20th August 2020.

Contents

Introduction

1. Crewe - The first major trainspotting adventure
2. Football and Old Trafford
3. Sheffield
4. Stockport and Woodley Junction
5. Shrewsbury and North Wales
6. School holiday to the Isle of Bute
7. Manchester and local North West Sheds
8. Leeds and York trips
9. Trainspotting Clubs and Societies
10. Britannia Locomotives
11. Family holidays to the South Coast and Popular Music
12. December 1967 to August 1968 – The final run down of steam
13. The preservation era
14. Life after school
15. Renewed interest in railways

Introduction

My name is Ian Cook, born in 1952 and for as long as I can remember I have had an interest in railways. It's these memories regarding my passion for railways that has inspired me to write my first book with the aim of providing an insight as to what some children and teenagers did before the days of computer games, mobile 'phones and Social Media. Basically, we got out and did things, like playing football, exploring unfamiliar places or enjoying a hobby, like trainspotting, stamp collecting, fishing, collecting sports cards and riding bikes, learning to play a musical instrument to name a few. I was fortunate that my home in Hyde, Cheshire, prior to our move to Woodley during 1963 was alongside a small farm, where we could play football on an adjoining farmer's field until late at night when it became too dark, we then took advantage of a nearby street light and used it as a floodlight.

My earliest memories of railways date back to the time when I went on holiday to my parent's caravan at Llanddulas in North Wales, fortunately our caravan was located alongside the main line from Chester to Llandudno and Holyhead. As soon as I was old enough, I would climb the embankment up to a stone wall that overlooked the main North Wales railway line and spend virtually all day there with my notebook and pen noting down every locomotive that passed by. By the summer of 1960, I had become totally hooked on the hobby of trainspotting, which at the time had a widespread interest amongst youngsters in my age group.

At about this time some famous steam locomotives were being employed on the crack expresses that used the North Wales coast, like Stanier Duchess's, Princess's, Royal Scots, Patriots and Jubilees. Duchess's and Princess's are classified as Pacifics locomotives, a steam Locomotive that had a wheel arrangement of 4-6-2: four leading wheels on two axles, six driving wheels on three axles and finally two trailing wheels on one axle. The trailing axle would generally be located under the cab of the locomotive. These Pacifics had been relegated to the North Wales Coast from their former duties on the West Coast Main Line (WCML) following the introduction of modern Type 4 diesels on the WCML. This provided the perfect opportunity for me to see these engines, which to be honest, I had virtually no chance of seeing back home. The much larger Pacifics would work the more glamorous services that were deemed important enough to have names associated with the service and the titled services operating along the North Wales Coast at this time included: The Emerald Isle Express, Irish Mail (A boat train) and the appropriately named 'Welsh Dragon' that operated from London Euston to Holyhead.

Our home in Hyde, Cheshire approximately 9 miles east of Manchester had a reasonable rail service. The nearest railway line to our home was about a ten-minute walk and as I gained sufficient courage, I would walk to the freight line that passed through Stockport and on to Godley Junction. I would perch myself on the fence and watch as the steam locomotives worked hard with their heavy freight trains that had either originated in Yorkshire or on Merseyside. Most of the engines on this route were either from Gorton or Heaton Mersey sheds and at the time many of these locomotives had an Eastern Region influence.

At about the same time, I would sometimes travel to my Dad's garage, which was virtually next to Newton station on the electrified route from Manchester to Sheffield. The highlight of these trips would be when the local pick-up freight arrived at Newton station from Gorton to carry out its shunting duties in the station yard. This would have been before my 10th birthday, so unfortunately, I never kept my notes as in those days you wrote down which engines you had seen then underlined them in your Ian Allan Locoshed. Ian Allan was an individual who first realised that there was a demand for books detailing the numbers of locomotives that operated on the British Railways Network. He began with the local area on the Southern Region but in time he eventually published books detailing the entire railway network. Once the engine was correctly underlined you threw away the notes that you had made of what you had seen that day. This changed by the time I had reached 12 when I began to maintain a record of the locomotives I saw, the location and sometimes the date.

One of my earliest memories of going to my Dad's garage was helping my Uncle Tom with his Bantam chickens, a miniature size chicken that laid tiny eggs. Uncle Tom was a Coal Merchant with his business located next to my Dad's garage. He had a background in farming prior to moving in to the coal business, so the hen house providing a home for the Bantams was really a hangover from his earlier years. Uncle Tom was an extremely slightly built man but his small stature didn't stop him being able to bag half a hundred weight of coal then swinging it in the air and dropping it onto the back of his coal lorry. By the age of 10, I was slightly taller than my Uncle and on one occasion thought I would help him bag some coal. Within about 15 minutes I was completely exhausted but still tried to swing the bag I had filled onto the back of his lorry, I failed miserably and Uncle Tom decided to continue unassisted.

It was around this time I bumped into a fellow trainspotter called Michael Theyer, who lived in Newton on Talbot Road and as a result of the catchment area, he attended a different school to me. We were both about the same age and had a similar interest in railways and would meet on the occasions I went to Newton station, which was much more frequent during school holidays. I still find it amazing how we managed to keep in contact as we went to different schools and lived several miles apart. Through our common interest in railways, we eventually became close friends and soon began to make plans for ventures further afield than our local stations.

I think the craziest thing we ever did together was during August 1965, prior to our return to school after the summer break. Without any sort of a plan, we set off one day and cycled from my home to visit a number of different engine sheds in the Manchester area. I think the day started off with Michael cycling to my place from his home in Newton, he had recently received a new bike with gears and all the bells and whistles. After a while, one of us must have suggested going for a bike ride around Manchester, not the brightest of ideas, even more so when you were 13 years old and to be honest neither of us had any knowledge of the road network in and around Manchester. But that is exactly what we did and neither of our parents had a clue what we were doing. If my daughters at the same age had done a similar thing, I would have blown a fuse but I suspect we were so consumed by our interest in railways that the dangers of cycling around Manchester never occurred to us.

We eventually set off cycling through Hyde on the main road into Manchester, our first shed was Gorton, which was at one time a huge railway complex comprising of a shed and railway works. Amazingly, we found the shed relatively easily but discovered the main entrance gate locked. After a short discussion, Michael agreed to climb over a sizeable wall that surrounded the shed complex, whilst I looked after the bikes. A good idea as Gorton at the time had a somewhat dodgy reputation, however in hindsight any potential thieves would have nicked Michaels new shiny bike but possibly left mine behind. Shortly after Michael returned to confirm our worst fears that the depot had closed, I have since found out it closed during June 1965. Not a good start to our cycling adventure. Next stop was Reddish shed which wasn't that far from Gorton and here we found fourteen EMI's electric locomotives and a single Brush Type 4 diesel, neither of us had ever been to Reddish before, so our first success. Then onto Longsight shed which was located alongside the main road that connected Hyde to Manchester so relatively easy to find. The shed was by then a modern diesel and electric depot with no steam locomotives present, other than a coal tender previously used on a Duchess Pacific, which I believe was being used as a water carrier. After this we started to head home, I started to experience a lot of pain from my saddle, which had virtually collapsed. Solution, Michael offered to let me use his bike whilst he struggled on mine, that's what you call true friendship. Surprisingly, we both made it home safely without any incidents and I believe neither of us mentioned a word to our respective parents regarding our cycling adventure. If we had, I suspect we would have been grounded for weeks! I have since discovered that neither my brother nor sister knew what we had got up to on that day! However, if I had owned a much more suitable bike, we would have almost certainly repeated the adventure and who knows where we would have finally ended up; Bury, Oldham or other sheds in the Manchester area.

EMI locomotives at Reddish Depot
At a much later date than the visit during our cycling adventure.

Early photo of Ann (sister), myself and Peter (Brother)

Crewe - The First Major Trainspotting Adventure

By June 1963, we had moved from Hyde to a new home in Woodley, which thankfully was even closer to the same railway line that I had been visiting in Hyde but a few miles closer to Stockport. The road that ran alongside the station at Woodley became my usual spotting haunt and I would be occasionally joined by Michael, who would cycle from his home in Newton to Woodley. At about the same time I had started at my new senior school, Greenfield Street Secondary Modern in Hyde. Soon after starting at Greenfield Street I overheard some older boys talking about going to the Crewe Sheds, which I thought they had said going to Creweshanks, which was a specialist dentist that I went to in Manchester with my mother, brother and sister. This confused me at the time but on asking why they were going to the same dentist, they enlightened me by saying they were planning on going to the railway sheds in Crewe not to Creweshanks the dentists, needless to say I felt slightly stupid but my confusion had opened up a huge opportunity for me. In those days, trainspotting was a fairly popular hobby for young boys and in some places, schools often had trainspotting clubs to help boys with their hobby. This unfortunately wasn't the case at either my school or the school that Michael went to, so we tended to make friends with those boys with the same interest. I was only 11 at the time, so I had never been anywhere other than local railway stations or railway lines that were nearby. So, the opportunity to go to a place like Crewe certainly got the brain cells working and my imagination went into overdrive. Crewe at the time was one of the main railway centres in the North West of England and had four sheds and a railway works where they repaired and built locomotives. All locomotives were assigned to a shed, where they were maintained and fuelled ready for their next duties. The four depots at Crewe included; Crewe North, Crewe South, Gresty Lane sub shed and the recently built diesel depot alongside Crewe station. I shall provide a better explanation of what sheds were later but the more urgent thing at the time was how on earth could myself and Michael convince our respective parents that we would be safe to travel from our homes to Crewe, which at the time might as well be on the other side of the planet. I suspect, both of us did a pretty good job of persuading our parents and they eventually agreed that we could go with the older boys. Saturday 5th October 1963 was the agreed date for the trip and we would catch the number 30 bus that passed through Hyde and Woodley and dropped you off on the approach to Stockport Edgeley station.

The excitement was off the scale and as a consequence I suspect I would have got very little sleep the night before the trip and definitely won't have needed my Dad to wake me in the morning. Thankfully, we all made it safely to Edgeley station and were soon on one of the new modern electric multiple units (EMU) that had recently taken over the stopping services from Manchester Piccadilly to Crewe, following the recent electrification of the main line south out of Manchester Piccadilly.

Soon after leaving Stockport Edgeley station we passed the shed at Stockport Edgeley to the right of the main line that stood alongside the football ground for Stockport County FC. I believe this was the first time myself and Michael had seen the shed which had a depot code of 9B. This shed code in those days was made from cast iron and bolted on the smoke box of the steam locomotives or on the cab of diesel or electric locomotives and indicated to the authorities where the locomotive was allocated to. It also helped trainspotters to know if they were seeing a rare locomotive that maybe visiting the area from further afield. Each of the sheds would have a unique code and were usually grouped by an area, so in the case of Stockport Edgeley, who's code was 9B, it was grouped together with other sheds in the Manchester area, with Longsight being the main shed with a code of 9A. Other sheds in the area included: Newton Heath (9D), Trafford Park (9E), Heaton Mersey, Stockport (9F) etc.

After quickly noting down as many of the locomotive numbers that could be seen on Edgeley shed, we were soon heading south towards our destination of Crewe. The journey took about 45 mins and as soon as we arrived in a bay platform at the north end of Crewe station, we were greeted with the magnificent sight of a Duchess Pacific about to depart on a special railtour to Edinburgh's Princess Street station. The Duchess was 46251 'City of Nottingham' which had been specially spruced up for the occasion. The railtour was called 'Duchess Commemorative Rail Tour' and had been arranged to allow enthusiasts to sample the joys of riding behind one of Sir William Stanier's infamous Pacific locomotives. These locomotives were quickly coming to the end of their working lives with virtually all their main duties now in the hands of diesel locomotives. It was fairly common practice for special rail tours to be organised for classes of locomotive that were soon to become extinct. In fact, the remaining operational Duchesses would all be finally withdrawn by October 1964 with the majority being sent for scrap at various scrapyards across the country. Fortunately, three members of the class were saved from the cutters torch: Duchess of Hamilton, Duchess of Sutherland and City of Birmingham.

After watching 'City of Nottingham' depart on its long journey north to Edinburgh, we walked to the end of the Platform that we had arrived on along with an army of other trainspotters and enthusiasts. From our vantage point we could easily see Crewe North shed which was just across from us at the side of the station. Crewe North had a code of 5A and was the main locomotive shed in the Crewe area and was responsible for maintaining the express passenger locomotives that worked that area of the WCML.

At the time, Crewe was a good a place as any to find many of the prestigious engines associated with the WCML including: Duchesses, Royal Scots, Patriots, Jubilees Britannia and the unique BR built 'Duke of Gloucester' plus many other less famous engines. There was a footbridge that lead from the furthest platform to the shed but unfortunately you had to walk past the Shed Foreman's office to gain entry via this route. Needless to say, it was illegal to visit most railway sheds on the rail network unless you had a permit to authorise entry, permits cost money and took time to acquire, so basically you tried your best to get around a shed without a permit.

Shed visits were an essential part of any trip and was by far the best way to see locomotives that may be being repaired and not in service or even stored or withdrawn from service awaiting their final journey to a breakers yard. This fact was becoming ever more common at the time as BR was in full swing to replace all its steam locomotives with either diesel and electric traction, resulting in hundreds of locomotives being withdrawn each month and by the time I was visiting Crewe, steam had virtually been eliminated from parts of Britain, especially the Western Region in particular Cornwall and Devon. The perilous fate of steam locomotives was even more obvious when we managed to get around Crewe North shed.

After spending an hour or two on the end of the platform watching dozens of trains arrive and depart Crewe station, the older boys decided it was time to head off towards the first shed visit, which was to be the relatively new Diesel Depot positioned at the side of the station and easy to reach by the service road that took you to the depot from the side of the station. It was whilst we were walking around the inside of the depot that myself and Michael got separated from the other older boys and we soon realised we were on our own. After quickly noting down the remaining numbers, we decided to head back to the station. Unfortunately, we didn't even realise there were two more steam sheds close by to the diesel depot. At the young age of 11, we just didn't have the knowledge regarding the layout of a place like Crewe, so the safest thing to do was to head back to the station. We soon plucked up sufficient courage to walk over the footbridge and into Crewe North shed. Luckily, we didn't see the Foreman or anybody else who may have told us off for trespassing. Our desire to record every locomotive on the shed just motivated us even more. Crewe North in those days was huge and comprised three main parts, a twelve road and four road dead end running shed, a series of sidings and an 8 road semi-roundhouse that was accessed from the shed turntable. At this time the area between the main running shed and the semi round house was where all the stored and withdrawn locomotives were located. I'd never seen so many named locomotives in my life, with masses of engines stored out of use awaiting their final journey to the scrapyard. To be honest at our young age you just didn't realise what was happening but had to record every single engine. We must have noted down in the region of a hundred locomotives by the time we were leaving the semi roundhouse and immediately headed in the direction of the footbridge and back to the safety of the station.

By now it was time for lunch, so we opened up our bags to enjoy the contents, which usually comprised of a number of sandwiches and a bottle of drink i.e., orange or similar. My bag in those days was an ex-army shoulder bag that kept loyal to me for many a year, I would dread to think how many sandwiches I stuffed into it over the years. One thing boys of my age weren't into in those days was fashion, so no designer or other fancy bags, just simple practical items like my ex-army bag and of course a Parka coat, which I seemed to wear no matter how hot or cold it was.

Around this time, we were re-joined by the older boys who immediately asked what had happened to us, I don't think they were too concerned but just being polite. They asked if we had managed to get around all four depots, to which we replied 'Four', thinking we had done well getting around two of them. The sight of what they had noted down on Crewe South and Gresty Lane somewhat put a dampener on things but that's life. Considering it was early October, the traffic passing through station was considerable and added to the fact that most of the freight passed via the smoke hole, which passed under Crewe North depot and was down a cutting at the side of the station made it difficult to see the freight on this route. This included most of the freight arriving from the north i.e., Liverpool, Manchester, Preston, Carlisle and Scotland. However, there was a huge amount of passenger and parcel traffic arriving and departing Crewe during the day. By mid-afternoon we watched our first ever Great Western steam engine arrive into the station from the south. It was a Grange class locomotive and had arrived with a parcel train from I suspect either Shrewsbury or more than likely the route that is now home to the Severn Valley Railway. We just couldn't believe our eyes as this was a truly alien engines to us, with all its highly polished brass and copper accessories, which appeared very impressive to boys from Manchester. I also recall a good number of Patriot steam locomotives were still operating passenger services at the time, within little over 12 months these engines would all be history and not a single example saved for preservation. However, that is about to change with the project to build a new Patriot class steam engine, which is now well on its way to delivering a newly built member of the class. The new locomotive will carry the name 'The Unknown Warrior', which is fitting as several members of the class carried the names of famous Army Regiments or the names of soldiers who were honoured by being awarded the Victoria Cross or similar.

One of the sounds that got many of the trainspotters excited whilst they were gathered together at the north end of Crewe station was the sound of a Pacific whistle as an engine was about to leave Crewe North shed. The whistle on most of the Pacific locomotives was generally a Chime whistle with a very distinctive sound. Indeed, during the afternoon that distinctive sound was heard and within minutes the glorious sight of the unique British Railways built three-cylinder Pacific 'Duke of Gloucester' appeared as it moved off Crewe North shed. Even though I had seen it several times before working along the North Wales coast, it was a sight to behold and obviously caused considerable excitement for those spotters gathered that day at Crewe.

One of the other activities that entertained us during our stay at Crewe was the sight of a small Jinty shunting locomotive going about its duties in the carriage sidings to the right of the line that arrived into Crewe from the Manchester direction. The little 0-6-0 shunting engine would burst out of the sidings pulling a number of coaches or parcel vans then slam on its brakes as it entered the furthest track at the right-hand side of the station. Because the crew hadn't bothered to connect the locomotive brakes to those on the carriages or vans and as a consequence were just using the locomotive brakes, which was insufficient to bring the train to a sudden halt, resulting in the engine and its train simply sliding into the station. The driver knew exactly when to apply the brake and how far his train would slide until it came to a halt. This action obviously didn't do the engines wheels any good and presumably would result in all the driving wheels on the Jinty looking more like threepenny bits (For those too young to remember pre decimalisation coins it's akin to a 50 pence coin).

Crewe station was a huge junction with effectively 6 routes merging into the station. These included three lines from north: North Wales/Chester, Liverpool/Carlisle/Scotland and Manchester. From the south side of the lines branched off to Stoke/Derby, London/Birmingham and Shrewsbury/Wales. Needless to say, with so many destinations, Crewe was an extremely busy station and attracted many hundreds of railway enthusiasts or as they were called in those days trainspotters.

By late afternoon we were heading back to Stockport, unfortunately on another EMU. Once again taking note of any visible locomotives on Stockport Edgeley shed. Then the bus back to Woodley where I said goodbye to Michael as he had to travel back to his home in Newton on the other side of Hyde.

The following day I spent hours neatly underlining all the numbers I had recorded from my notebook into my Ian Allan Locoshed Book. This book was the equivalent of a bible to a young trainspotter in those days and basically enabled an individual to clearly identify which locomotives they had seen and more importantly those that they hadn't! The underlined numbers were those you had seen, plus you could add other notes like write a 'C' next to those engines that you had 'cabbed', this was another peculiar habit that trainspotters had in those days, the need to stand in the cab of a locomotive, it certainly was a good idea during the freezing winter months whilst standing on a cold damp platform, and you were offered the opportunity of instant warmth following a quick visit to the hot cab of a locomotive. The Locoshed book would also give you a good idea if you had seen any rare engines like the GWR Grange locomotive I saw at Crewe. In addition to the Locoshed book, which was handy pocket size book costing in the region 2 shillings and sixpence in 1963, there was also the Ian Allan Combined Volume book, which provided much more detail about each class of locomotive i.e., weight, wheel arrangements, names etc. The Combined Volume was a hard-back book which contained photographs of many of the classes of engines and cost considerably more at 12 shillings and sixpence. Finally, there was the British Locomotive Shed Directory, which provided a complete guide to the location of all main BR sheds and how to reach them from the nearest station or local bus stop. This book cost three shillings and sixpence and was an essential guide if the shed wasn't too close to the nearest station, in many cases it provided bus routes for those sheds further afield. Finally, with regard to these books, trainspotters would care for them as if their life depended on it and in many cases, they would wrap a paper cover over the outside of the book to protect it from any possible damage. Another useful thing to do, was write your name and address on the inside sheet of the book, in case you accidentally lost the book, which in my case did happen and a very kind person actually posted the book back to me.

Unfortunately, I never kept my notebook from my first trip to Crewe, so I'm unable to look back accurately at what we had seen, other than the knowledge the numbers were all underlined in my Ian Allan books. By early 1964, I started to maintain a much better record of what I had seen but not always the actual date, this record keeping became better within a short period of time and by the end of my spotting days when steam was coming to an end, I would record if the locomotive was in steam, what it was working or if it was stored or withdrawn.

As an indication of how excited I was with the trip to Crewe, a little later after the trip I asked my Dad if he had any large pieces of paper to enable me to draw a detailed plan of the layout of Crewe station. The only paper available which would enable me to produce such a layout was the reverse side of some wallpaper. So, wallpaper it had to be and with a long ruler and various pencils I began to draw a layout of the station, including all the platforms, foot bridges and tracks that passed through the station, including the sidings that the Jinty used to reverse into whilst shunting its coaches and also recording the position of the footbridge from the furthest platform to a path that lead to Crewe North shed. I must admit that was a one off and don't recall what happened to my drawing but yet another example of my enthusiasm/obsession for railways.

Another interest at the time was my Art work, which largely involved railway scenes and was encouraged by my parents who on my birthday or at Christmas bought me fairly large sketch books to complete my drawings. Even though I say it myself, I certainly developed a talent for art, so much so that I managed to get a Grade 1 in Art for my GCSE and O Level exams. The latter involved me displaying my work at the nearby Flowery Field school, where officials could examine your work and award your final grades. My Art teacher at the time was young and had a serious interest in more abstract work, whether that be on paper or producing a sculpture or similar. After numerous attempts by him to change my approach to creating my own drawings or paintings, he finally gave up but then taught me how to use colours to develop a scene, which I must admit I did take on board. We were allowed to leave school if we required to draw or paint a scene outside the school grounds, needless to say some boys just took advantage of this and just disappeared for the duration of the lesson, whilst I actually used the opportunity to develop my work and would usually be found on a platform at the local Hyde Central railway station where I began to draw scenes of a very dilapidated station, which was perfect preparation for the main work, required for my examinations. I can't remember the Art teacher's name but he really did help me in the use of colours plus the textures the colours could form and finally resulted in my main work being considered good enough to be awarded the top grade for my O Level Art examination.

Another subject I thoroughly enjoyed was Technical Drawing, which was taught by my teacher Mr Wainwright, who had a renowned track record of being a disciplinarian, so not a person to take lightly. Again, like my Art work I also gained a top grade at GCSE and O level examinations for Technical Drawing. With my appreciation of work involving the Arts, I started to think along the lines of training to become an Architect but my only encounter with a Careers advisor during my final year soon removed any thoughts I had of doing that as a career. I honestly think the career advisor thought you are at a secondary modern school with a poor academic record, so you need to be thinking of something a little less exciting; like working in a shop or in the building trade. I would love to have met the guy six years later when I graduated from Salford University. I honestly believe he also thought I had no chance of getting a job in the aviation industry. So, my advice to any youngster reading this, don't let some old fool or so-called expert discourage you from doing what you really want to do. That is, as long as your objectives are achievable, which might involve years of studying and hard work!

Football and Old Trafford

Another major interest of mine at the time was football, whether this was playing or watching football. Up to the time of my first visit to Crewe I had only been to watch my local team; Hyde United and this usually involved sneaking into the ground via a gap in one of the dodgy fences that surrounded the ground. As Hyde played none league football and the crowd was never that large the ground staff just turned a blind eye to our presence on the far terracing built from dirt and old railway sleepers with no form of covered stand to provide shelter on those dark wet days back in the early 1960's.

However, a couple of weeks after my amazing trip to Crewe, I was playing around in the back garden at home, in fact I had climbed on top of the garage, which was built with corrugated sheets of steel and curved in shape, so not the easiest place to climb on top off. Whilst I was on top of the garage a school friend; Peter King, who lived about three doors further along, shouted to me 'Do you fancy going to see United today', to which I replied, 'Hyde United'? 'No' he replied, 'Manchester United'. My dad wants to know if you fancy coming with us, to which I yelled 'Yes' and simply jumped off the top of the garage and legged it up the steps into the house to see if I was allowed. To be honest I could have easily broken my legs by jumping off the garage but the thought of seeing my first game at Old Trafford, simply took over, amazingly my Mum agreed and I quickly got ready and ran around to Peter's house.

The date was Saturday 26th October 1963 and West Ham United were the visitors to Old Trafford. At the time West Ham United had some very famous players including: Bobby Moore, Martin Peters and Geoff Hurst, all of whom would play a major part in England winning the World Cup during 1966. However, Manchester United were still rebuilding the team following the Munich air disaster but still had legends like; Bobby Charlton, Dennis Law, Nobby Stiles and the new boy we had recently bought from Arsenal and former Stockport County player; David Herd, in fact, I believe it was David's first game following his transfer.

In those days not many people owned cars, so it was public transport for us, a quick walk into Hyde to catch a bus from Hyde bus station into Manchester Piccadilly then one of the huge number of buses provided to get fans to Old Trafford. I still remember the scene on Chester Road in Old Trafford where our bus pulled up to allow the fans to get off. The whole of Chester Road was overflowing with double deck buses and thousands of fans milling about, heading to the ground. The main thing for me to do was stay close to Peter and his Dad, as I was not going to miss the game through being overwhelmed by the occasion and getting lost in the ground.

We managed to make it to the ground and Peters Dad chose to enter the south stand, that's the stand nearest the railway line. We stood in the paddock close to the edge of the playing field and the first thing I noticed was that everyone appeared to have red and white scarves and wooden football rattles, these were a hand-held device that made a deafening sound when thousands of fans were using them. As the players came onto the pitch from a point very close to where we were standing the whole ground erupted with fans twirling their scarves and rattles around in the air above their heads. I'd never in my short life seen anything quite like it and certainly massively topped the noise created by the two hundred or so fans at Hyde United ground!

The match wasn't the best I'd seen and basically both sides appeared to cancel one another out in midfield. So, by the time we left the ground with about four or five minutes remaining the score was still 0-0. Peters Dad, decided it was important we leave before the bulk of the forty-five thousand fans decided to leave. We made it safely onto one of the multitude of buses waiting on Chester Road then into Piccadilly for our bus back to Hyde. I hope I adequately thanked Peters Dad but the occasions may have been too much to remember such pleasantries. Anyway, I was extremely fortunate and hope I did indeed thank him properly. We were all of the belief that the score was 0-0, until I walked into my home, only to be told by my Dad, 'Don't worry son, I'm sure they will win next time you go'! Yes, West Ham United had scored right at the death, so late we must have been heading into Manchester on the bus and didn't even hear the crowd's reaction to the late goal.

Once I started at the senior school at Greenfield street, I visited Old Trafford many more time, none more so than when I went to Salford University, as a number of mates from the Mechanical Engineering school were football fans and didn't mind who they went to watch as long as it was a good game. Strangely enough the final year at University was when Manchester United had been relegated into the second division. The previous season when we were scheduled to play Manchester City on the last home game of the season at Old Trafford, our former striker Dennis Law famously back heeled the ball into the United net at the Score Board end of Old Trafford following a corner that was taken from where I was standing. Thankfully, Dennis didn't celebrate but he had in fact done United a big favour and enabled a proper rebuild of the team which would in turn enable a quick return to the top tier of English Football.

This would be United first season in the second tier since 1937-38 but interestingly a number of other so-called big named clubs also found themselves in the same predicament, namely Nottingham Forest, Sheffield Wednesday, Aston Villa and Sunderland. The attendance at most of the matches at Old Trafford was unbelievable and confirmed the loyalty of the fans. Virtually all the remaining games had attendances in excess of fifty thousand. Their average attendance that season was over 47,700, which was the highest average attendance for any club in English football including the whole of the first division.

The home game that did stand out was on Saturday 30th November 1974 when Sunderland were the visitors. Old Trafford at the time apparently had a crowd limit of 59,500 but the official figures on the day confirm that at least 60,500 got into the ground. We usually stood in the United Road paddock but had been forced from our usual position close to the half way line into the corner next to the Stretford End and to be honest I have never felt so uncomfortable as that day at Old Trafford. I suspect they had allowed many more fans than the official figures and we were all packed liked sardines. Thankfully, Sunderland came to try and win and didn't at any point sit back and defend and the game turned out to be one of those classic encounters, with United winning 3-2. To be honest Sunderland deserved a point as they certainly came to battle it out with the Red Devils.

At the end of the season Tommy Docherty had rebuilt the team that was more committed to attacking football, which is what the crowds at Old Trafford wanted. They ended their first season back at the top flight in third position with an average home attendance of over fifty-three thousand with almost Sixty-two thousand attending the home game against Everton. I attended most of the home games with my good friend from work Tony Kelso and his wife, the only problem was that most of the home games became all ticket and you had to make sure you had sufficient tokens from the United football programs to have any chance of getting tickets. This was the start of the time when it became seriously difficult to obtain tickets and also the time when season ticket sales took off, making it even harder for the average fan who just wanted to see them when they had time available and more importantly couldn't afford to buy a season ticket.

The rest is now history and days of Old Trafford being full of local supporters has been and gone, with huge numbers of visitors from abroad regularly attending the home games at Old Trafford. I remember a fairly recent visit to Old Trafford when after the game I was stood at the Tram Stop at Old Trafford and all I good hear was the sound of Scandinavians chatting around me, well at least it makes a change from hearing the dulcet tones of Mancunians.

Old Trafford today is a far cry from those early days in the 1960's when the Score board end was completely open with no cover provided for those hardy fans who decided to stand in the open. As its name suggests it was also the place where the half time scores of the other league games would appear. No fancy electronic score board, just a wooden frame where they would simply hang a board displaying the half time score of the other matches being played. This would allow you check on the progress of some of the teams you were competing against in the league. If my memory serves me right the half time scores would have a letter hung with each score, you would then check in the Match Programme the game against each letter e.g. A 1-0 would indicate the score for the first game listed in the programme. Another highlight of half time was the chance to get a cup of hot Bovril, a life saver during those harsh winter months.

In more recent times I've been treated to an Old Trafford full hospitality package the following is on one of those occasions on the 27th October 2007 when United beat Middlesbrough 4-1 with a crowd in excess of Seventy-five thousand.

Myself and two colleagues from Higher Education
Duncan and Janet with the Premier League Trophy

Sheffield

By early 1964, we had decided to venture to another new location and chose Sheffield as a suitable place to visit. I think our selection was based on the fact that it was easily accessible from where we lived as there was a regular service from Manchester Piccadilly to Sheffield Victoria via the former Woodhead route. Many of these services stopped at Guide Bridge station, which was easy to reach for both of us. The service was hauled by British Railways built EM1 or EM2 electric locomotives which were introduced during the mid-1950's on the newly electrified route using a 1500 DC power supply. Which was completely different power supply to that selected for the new electric route from Manchester to Crewe i.e., 25 kV AC. Prior to our trip we made some enquiries into the cost of the return ticket, to make sure we could afford it.

By this time both Michael and myself had paper rounds, this helped with the cost of buying tickets to enable us to explore more of the BR network. Unfortunately, I was given a paper round that involved morning and afternoon deliveries from Monday to Saturday plus the huge Sunday morning delivery. My Sunday paper round was so large, I started off with one fully packed bag and half way around the owner of the paper shop would drop off another fully packed bag for me to complete my round. Annoyingly if I wanted to take a Saturday off, the owner of the shop gave me considerable grief for asking to take time off and all I got for a full week's work was 15 shillings, about the cost of a return to Crewe. One of the main reasons we couldn't afford too many trips to places further afield than Stockport or Manchester.

Saturday the 8th February 1964 was the date we agreed to visit Sheffield and we did opt to travel from Guide Bridge to Sheffield Victoria, as we weren't aware there was an alternative route from Manchester Central to Sheffield Midland station that stopped at Romiley station. Romiley was just one stop further up the line from Woodley and at this time had a regular steam hauled service to Sheffield from Manchester Central station, more than likely hauled by an Eastern Region Class B1 locomotive.

The coaches on the Woodhead route were old compartment stock with a corridor that connected the compartments. We were joined by an older man who immediately fell asleep. The service only stopped at Penistone after departure from Guide Bridge before arriving at Sheffield Victoria station. The guy who had fallen asleep was still asleep on our arrival, so being polite, I gently woke him up, he immediately asked where we were, so I told him! He then had the nerve to tell me off as he wanted to get off at Penistone! First lesson learnt; don't be helpful and wake people up when you are on a train as you may get a load of hassle for your kindness. It would have been interesting to know, if I hadn't have woken him up, could he have gone all the way back to Manchester Piccadilly station. Can you just picture the look on his face!

We soon found out that Sheffield Victoria station had a very limited rail service with its main passenger service being the one we had earlier travelled on and both of us didn't need any of the EM1 or EM2 locomotives. The only locomotives we found of interest was those that worked freight services which included a couple of LNER B1's: 61120 and 61127 plus our first former Great Central Railways O4, which dated back to 1918 i.e., 63902. By lunch time we had visited the station buffet bar numerous times as we were getting bored with the lack of train activity. But then we had a stroke of luck and bumped into some local kids who asked us if we knew what was going on at Sheffield Midland station, to which we replied 'Sheffield Midland station where's that?'. Thankfully they took us over to Midland station, where we soon realised most of the passenger services operated from, including all the trains to London St Pancras and those to Manchester Central. We saw twice as much in two hours at Midland than we had done all morning at the Victoria station. By this time most of the London services were in the hands of modern Peak diesels but there was sufficient steam engine activity including the departure of LMS Jubilee 45675 'Hardy' on what I now suspect was a Manchester Central service. Needless to say, we could have returned on this but as two uninformed 11-year-olds we opted to travel back from Victoria station. The only bonus of this route was that we noticed a former Gresley designed K3; 61950 waiting to be cut-up at Cox and Danks Scrapyard at Wadsley Bridge, Sheffield. Thankfully, we didn't encounter any more grumpy old passengers on our return journey.

As youngster we never thought of obtaining any British Railways Timetables or even if these were available to purchase. The lack of any Timetables was the reason we didn't know that some routes had alternatives, like Manchester to Sheffield was a good example. I recently purchased a number of British Railway Timetables for the London Midland Region via E-Bay, which included most of the services in and around Manchester. These timetables covered the period we both started to travel beyond our local area. However, with no Timetables to help us with our travel plans we would find the time to closely examine the departure timetables on display at stations like Guide Bridge and Stockport in attempt to try and discover other destination that were available to us. This is basically why Crewe and Sheffield were the first places we visited.

Stockport and Woodley Junction

Soon after moving to Woodley during 1963 I started to walk from my new home across to a nearby railway line between Bredbury and Romiley stations, a walk of about 30 minutes. This location included four tracks, the top two being the line from Manchester Piccadilly to Marple and New Mills and beyond. The lower two tracks were on the line from Manchester Central to Sheffield and Derby. It was the latter route that provided the most interesting services with a mixture of steam and diesels on the passenger services to and from Manchester Central. At this time the steam services were usually in the hands of LNER B1's or LMS Jubilees. It was during these visits that I bumped into more local trainspotters who told me about the shed at Stockport Edgeley and the fact that a former Edgeley Jubilee 45732 'Sanspareil' was withdrawn at the rear of the shed and would soon be on its final journey to a scrapyard in Yorkshire. They also helped in providing details of the bus service from Woodley that would drop you off relatively close to the shed.

Using the advice from the local spotters, on the 12th February 1964, I made my first trip using the number 30 bus from Woodley to Stockport Edgeley with the bus stopping close to the shed entrance. A cinder path lead down to the depot and on my first visit found approximately twenty-five engines on the depot. Edgeley had a fairly large allocation that included various types of engine including: tank engines, Crabs, Black 5's, 8F's and Jubilees plus visiting engines, typically WD's and B1's from sheds in Yorkshire. After my visit to Edgeley shed, I would usually walk across Stockport to the other station at Tiviot Dale to view two passenger services from Manchester Central to Sheffield and Derby via Buxton. Since acquiring the London Midland Region timetables for the period that I first started my visits to Stockport Tiviot Dale station, I have discovered I could have travelled on either of the two passenger services as both stopped at Romiley station. Then I would have simply caught a local stopping service from Romiley to Woodley. This obviously would have been much more interesting than using the bus to get home.

During my second visit to Edgeley shed on the 4th March 1964, I found the Jubilee 'Sanspareil' in sidings at the rear of the depot, which I hadn't discovered during my first visit. Jubilees were mainly used on express or semi fast passenger services and were usually maintained in spotless condition to present a good image to the passengers using these services. However, by the time of my visit, 'Sanspareil' had lost all its glamour and was by then in a very poor external condition and was the first Jubilee locomotive that I'd seen, deemed beyond economic repair and was assigned for scrapping.

Occasionally after a visit to Edgeley depot I would walk down to Heaton Mersey shed with the shed code of 9F. The reason for not visiting Heaton Mersey too frequently was the fact that it supplied the majority of the engines that worked the freight services through Woodley towards Godley. My first visit to Heaton Mersey shed took place on the 1st April 1964 and found a relatively full depot comprising the following class's: Ivatt Moguls known as Flying Pigs, Crabs, Stanier Black 5's and 8F's, Standard 9F's plus a couple of Fairburn tanks that were frequently used on banking duties on the freights, owing to the fairly steep gradients from Stockport Tiviot Dale to Woodley. To gain entry into Heaton Mersey depot, you had to cross a very narrow footbridge that crossed the River Mersey; as it ran alongside the depot. These days there is no sign that the depot ever existed, with a section of the M60 motorway occupying part of the shed site plus the freight lines that ran alongside the depot. Towards the end of the steam operation at Heaton Mersey, BR made the decision to build a diesel refuelling point between the former steam shed and freight lines. This facility didn't last too long and was eventually closed and I believe the building's steel structure was acquired by the Dinting Railway Centre and erected at the new preservation centre on the outskirts of Glossop.

Most weekends I would visit the shed at Stockport Edgeley, unless my finances allowed me to venture further afield. Plus, I also had to try and persuade the owner of the paper shop to allow me the odd Saturday off paper round duties, if I went to places like Crewe, Sheffield or Leeds etc. However, I could do both my morning and afternoon Saturday paper round if I only visited local sheds in the Stockport or Manchester area.

The range and type of locomotives that turned up at Stockport Edgeley depot was sometimes surprising with the sheds in Yorkshire sometimes allowing

LNER K1's to venture as far west as Stockport, twice I recorded K1's on Edgeley shed i.e., 62010 and 62060. The majority of freight from Yorkshire was handled by WD's or LNER B1's plus by the mid 1960's freight originating on Merseyside was often handled by the huge BR Standard 9F's. A regular freight diagram from Merseyside to Leeds involved a heavy Oil tanks service that frequently required a pair of Standard 9F's or a 9F paired with a Stanier Black 5 or 8F. This service I presume originated at the Shell Stanlow refinery and would be routed via the former Cheshire lines that passed the shed at Edgeley, where the steam locomotives would take on more water prior to their journey across the Pennines. The sight of a pair of BR Standard 9F's setting off from a water stop, proved to be spectacular as both engines would desperately try to restart their journey with such a heavy load.

Edgeley shed had an allocation of small tank engines during the early 1960's including Fowler designs, Ivatt 2MT's which were eventually replaced by a number of BR Standard 2MT class 84000 series tanks, these didn't last too long and soon made their way on to the scrap line at the rear of the shed. There were rumours that these tank engines were going to be used on the Isle of Wight to replace the 1889 built Adams O2 tanks engines used on the island but nothing came of it and the 84000's all went for scrap.

84013, 84017, 84019, 84025 and 84026 all withdrawn
At the rear of Edgeley shed – 6th March 1966.

Edgeley shed will be best remembered for its Jubilees and Britannias. The former included the now preserved Jubilee 45596 'Bahamas' but it was not unusual to find a number of Jubilee's on the shed. On the 11th Sept 1964 the following were on shed: 45562, 45596, 45654 and 45726. With the rundown of steam accelerating, BR took the unusual decision to allocate a number of Britannias to 9B as late as June 1965, these included 70004, 70015, 70021, 70026 and 70044. The idea was to use the Brits on express parcel services between Yorkshire and Stockport and they remained at Edgeley for around two years before being transferred away to Carlisle or in the case of 70026 'Polar Star' and 70044 'Earl Haig' both being withdrawn whilst allocated to 9B. I still remember the sight of 'Earl Haig' dumped on the scrap line at the rear of the shed and took a photograph of it there (see photograph in Chapter 10). Towards the end of steam, Edgeley shed held an impromptu Open Day on the 16th March 1968 when 45596 'Bahamas', 4472 'Flying Scotsman' and 70013 'Oliver Cromwell' were gathered together at the sidings at the rear of the shed. Many visiting engines would be serviced at Edgeley prior to them being involved in railtour duties in and around Manchester, these included: 35026, 60019, 61994 (3442) 70013 and 70038.

About, a year after moving to our new home in the middle of new estate in Woodley, we were once again on the move to a house on the same estate but located in the corner of the estate which had the advantage that my bedroom window at the rear of the house overlooked the railway line from Stockport. By this time the line from Merseyside was fairly busy with freight plus the odd passenger train during Bank holidays.

Unfortunately, the railway line was just too far away to be able to read the numbers on the front of steam locomotives from my bedroom. To overcome this problem, my Dad gave me a fairly large brass telescope with a maritime provenance. By placing the telescope out of one of the small opening windows, I could usually make out the number on the smoke box, unless the number plate had been removed. The other problem was if the steam locomotive was working in reverse and had its tender leading first. That apart, the telescope proved to be a very useful tool, until the day I accidentally dropped it out of the window whilst it was being balanced precariously. Needless to say, the fall didn't do the telescope any good and resulted in damage to one of the inner lenses. I made sure that my Dad didn't become aware of my accident but he must have been puzzled why all of a sudden, I was rushing out of the house sprinting down a short path to the road that overlooked the railway. The one line I couldn't see from my bedroom, was the line to Romiley, which was generally used by the local DMU service to Marple and Hayfield but did see the odd freight service. However, for about a year after our move I did occasionally see a steam hauled passenger service on the line to Romiley, always with a Hughes designed Crab locomotive and suspect it was a rush hour service to Hayfield with locomotive coming off Gorton shed with the service starting from Manchester Piccadilly.

45407 passing Woodley station 14th Feb 1967

Shrewsbury and North Wales

By March 1964, we were obviously both getting bored with our regular visits to Stockport, so we started to discuss other possible places of interest to visit. Michael suggested Doncaster but after making enquires at Guide Bridge station regarding the cost of a return ticket, it appeared the cost of a return ticket was far too expensive for us 12-year-olds. I suspect that the ticket office at Guide Bridge may have given Michael the cost of an adult return as I'm sure he was quoted a price considerably more than £1. Subsequently, we discovered that we could get to Shrewsbury on a service from Stockport via Crewe and after making enquires at Edgeley station we found we could afford a return ticket. So, purely on cost grounds, Shrewsbury was to be our next destination and with it being a former Great Western Region (GWR) shed, we both let our imagination run wild. Both of us had seen plenty of pictures of GWR engines with them adorned with brass and copper trimmings, that made them look even more special. In addition, we could stop off for a short time at Crewe station.

So, on the 8th April 1964 we once again set off on one of our adventures, after meeting up at Stockport Edgeley station. We headed south passing Stockport Edgeley shed and noted a Yorkshire visitor in the shape LNER B1 61189. We waited a short time at Crewe noting down Britannia locomotive 70027 'Rising Star', which at the time was a Holyhead based engine. After Crewe we would have seen Crewe South shed for our first time but were unable to record many engines as the shed was a distance to the left of the line to Shrewsbury. We obviously didn't consider looking on the other side of the line as we would have passed right alongside Crewe Gresty Lane shed and at that time, more than likely would have contained a number of Great Western engines. I believe we travelled to Shrewsbury from Crewe on a Diesel Multiple Unit (DMU). On our approach to Shrewsbury, we noticed a small group of locomotives stored at Harlescott siding to the right as you approached the station. This group comprised withdrawn Ivatt 2MT tank engines 41240 and 41203 with a former GWR County class locomotive positioned in between the two tank engines and to make matters worse the County had its smoke box and cab numbers removed plus no nameplate to enable us to identify it. It took me many years of research to discover which County class locomotive it was and now believe it was 1005 'County of Devon', which was one of the last County's to be withdrawn from Shrewsbury, where it had been in store for almost a year.

Soon after our arrival at Shrewsbury we began to see our first GWR engines with a number of GWR Granges, a Manor and 3826 a 2-8-0 freight engine from South Wales. However, I still have a vivid memory of the sight of LMS Jubilee 45699 'Galatea' running light engine past the huge Signal Box at the south end of Shrewsbury station presumably heading towards the depot. This engine was withdrawn from Shrewsbury shed during November 1964 and luckily made its way to the famous Dai Woodhams scrapyard at Barry Island, South Wales, where it stayed until April 1980. It was the 113th locomotive to leave the scrapyard and most enthusiasts thought it was going to be used as a parts donor for the repair of other steam locomotives. The reason for this, was that 'Galatea' was in an appalling condition, with its centre driving wheels sliced in half by a cutters torch to prevent it derailing whilst engines were moved about within the scrapyard. In addition, the salty sea air at Barry Island had taken a huge toll on the body of the locomotive. Galatea is now part of the fleet of steam locomotives used by West Coast Railways based at Carnforth and I've had the pleasure of riding behind it on a number of occasions in recent years. It's another fine example of how railway enthusiasts never know when to give up on a project no matter how impossible the task appears.

After an hour or so on the station, we decided to use our Ian Allan Shed Directory for the first time to locate the shed. We hadn't passed the shed on our arrival, so we knew it had to be somewhere south of the station. The Shed Directory was perfect with its description of how to walk to the shed from the station and within twenty-five minutes we were walking up the narrow path into the shed. The first engine was saw was a small GWR Pannier tank going about its shunting duties within the shed yard. Shrewsbury shed at the time had a shed code of 6D following its transfer from a GWR to a London Midland and Scottish (LMS) shed, it was previously classified as 89A. since 1960. The depot had two distinct parts, the former GWR shed which comprised 8 roads with an attached roundhouse, the other shed was a former London and North Western Railways (LNWR) shed with 9 roads. We immediately, started our walk around both parts of the shed and noted down 34 locomotives including two diesels, so the shed was still largely an active steam shed with an equal mixture of GWR and LMS designs plus some more modern British Railways built Standard type steam locomotives.

After completing our tour of the whole shed, we started our walk back to the station and spent several hours there before heading home. During the afternoon, we recorded two GWR Castles: 5055 'Earl of Eldon' and 5056 'Earl of Powis' on what I believe were Paddington to Birkenhead services. GWR Castles were by then the premier steam engine on the GWR following the withdrawal of all the Kings, but even Castles by this time were getting difficult to see, especially working on a passenger service. Our visit to Shrewsbury proved to be a very enjoyable day, so much so, we arranged a second visit during September of the same year. I can't remember what we travelled back to Crewe on but it was definitely a loco hauled service as I remember hanging out of a window on the return in an attempt to see if we passed any south bound services. Needless to say, about the only thing that we passed was a passenger train hauled by a Jubilee class locomotive and I somehow managed to miss its number.

When we arrived back at Crewe, we immediately headed over to Crewe North shed which was relatively empty compared with our previous visit in 1963. Just five Duchesses: 46228, 46240, 46243, 46251 and 46254 plus seven Brits: 70012, 70015, 70022, 70024, 70032, 70033 and 70050 along with Royal Scot 46155 and one Patriot 45534. I think this was the start of the decline of the North Shed, which would finally result in it being closed during 1965. Its destruction came as a massive surprise to me and Michael when we visited Crewe soon after it had been demolished, leaving a small diesel stabling point.

After safely negotiating the shed at Crewe North, we headed back to Stockport and noted nine locomotives on Edgeley shed including more visitors from Yorkshire: 61115, 90173, 90359 and 90620, before catching the bus home.

Later in the month on the 18th April 1964, I saw the famous Flying Scotsman for the first time when it passed through Newton station whilst working a Stephenson Locomotive Society special from Manchester Central to London Marylebone. It was obviously an important occasion as the local evening newspaper 'The Manchester Evening News' printed an article about it leaving Manchester that day. The main part of the article was about a man who had been taking photographs of it as it departed, forgetting he actually had a ticket to ride on the special, now that's when you know your passion for railways has got slightly out of control! I believe it was the last steam engine to work through Woodhead tunnel, albeit with assistance from an electric Class EM1 locomotive in both directions whilst passing through the tunnel.

During May 1964, my parents decided on a quick trip down to the caravan at Llanddulas in North Wales. Fortunately for me, whilst we were there, I saw recently preserved former London North Eastern Railways (LNER) K4 class 61994 'The Great Marquess' working a special from Leeds to Llandudno. The other bonus regarding this visit to North Wales, was I somehow managed to persuade my Dad to stop off at Mold shed on the return home. We would pass the shed at Mold every time my Dad drove to and from the caravan, along the former North Wales coast road. This was a very rare occasion, so I made the most of it and recorded all 32 engines that were on the depot, including two GWR Hall's 5984 'Linden Hall' and 6903 'Belmont Hall'. The shed was mainly full of Stanier designed locomotives; Black 5's and 8F's plus a single Jubilee 45606 'Falkland Islands' and a couple of small Jinty shunting engines 47350 and 47673.

Later that summer during June, we had two separate visits to the caravan, the first visit must have been a flying visit, as I only record 16 numbers during the visit, including Jubilee 45663 'Jervis', which was allocated to Speke Junction shed at the time, so suspect it was on a holiday extra from Liverpool. The second visit must have been for a full week, as I recorded 101 numbers during the visit. The bulk of the services were still worked by steam but the new English Electric Type 4 diesels were beginning to make significant inroads in to the services along the North Wales coast. The big surprise of this trip was the appearance of Sheffield Canklow based B1 61051, which worked a

Sheffield to Llandudno summer holiday extra on Saturday 20th June 1964. At this time the line that ran alongside the caravan site still had four tracks owing to the huge number of specials that worked during the summer months. From my vantage point on a stone wall overlooking the railway line I could see all the way around the bay past Abergele and Rhyl and it was not unusual to see at least one train at some point along the coast line. It must have been fairly relaxing for my parents with the knowledge that I would be sat in my usual place, frequently with a friend from the Midlands. At meal times, I would be summoned down to the caravan and would always sit in the seat with the best view of the railway line, in attempt to avoid missing anything. The range of locomotives that I recorded during this holiday was still very impressive, including one Patriot 45530, three Jubilees 45580, 45600 and 45633, six Brits 70003, 70005, 70024, 70026, 70042 and 70050 plus a stack of Patricroft based BR Standard Class 5's and of course the visitor from Yorkshire 61051. The other unusual sight was the number of tank engines that I recorded, including two Ivatt 2MT's 41220 and now preserved example 41241 plus 42240, 42489 and BR Standard tank 80102, which was allocated to Bangor shed for the period of the summer 1964 before heading back to Shrewsbury. I think that this was an Indian summer for steam hauled services along the North Wales coast as in subsequent years diesels made further inroads into the summer services and by the summer of 1967, steam had been totally eliminated and the formation reduced to just two tracks.

For the follow up trip to Shrewsbury during September 1964, I took my recently acquired Kodak Brownie camera, which I believe my Dad had given me, possibly for my 12th Birthday. For the very first time, I had the opportunity to take a limited number of photographs of mainly GWR engines that were at the front of the shed. Unfortunately, at a later date I accidentally dropped the camera whilst I was at Bournemouth station during a family holiday, resulting in most of the photos being damaged by light incursion, caused by a crack in the camera plastic body. However, some of the first photos taken at Shrewsbury shed weren't completely destroyed and clearly show a pair of GWR Hall Class locomotives; 6934 alongside 6922 at the front of the shed.

GWR Halls 6934 'Beachamwell Hall' and 6922 'Burton Hall'
At Shrewsbury shed on 19th September 1964

On the 4th June 1966, we discovered that the famous locomotive 'Flying Scotsman' would be passing the caravan with a special train from Lincoln Central to Llandudno. On the day I tried to photograph it passing the caravan site at Llanddulas but the results were very poor. Fortunately, my Dad offered to take me to Llandudno later in the afternoon to see it. The following photograph was taken by my dad on his Ensign Selfix-420 camera, this was a British built camera with a lens that folded out from within the camera body and had a Carl Zeiss Jena Tessar F4.5 lens. With a range of shutter speeds, the camera could produce a good quality photograph, clearly obvious from the photograph of the Scotsman at Llandudno station.

LNER A3 4472 at Llandudno station on 4th June 1966
My Dad's photograph.

My Dads Ensign Selfix-420 camera
With Lens open and ready for operation.

One of the other memories I have of being at the caravan was the problem of line side fires caused by steam engines, usually following a long dry spell. On one occasion late in the evening one steam engine that was being worked hard by its driver, managed to set fire to most of the vegetation alongside the track and the resulting fires could clearly be seen all around the bay. The fires became so bad that many of people staying at our camp site at the time helped to try and put out the fires with anything that came to hand.

School holiday to the Isle of Bute

During my first year at Greenfield Street Secondary Modern school, I found out that the school proposed to offer pupils the chance of a school holiday to the Isle of Bute in Scotland. The Isle of Bute is located on the west coast of Scotland, further down from the Clyde estuary and in those days a popular destination for holiday makers, especially those organised for school parties. This normally wouldn't have appealed to me until I found out that they planned to use the train to get to Scotland. This certainly caught my interest but I somehow had to convince my parents that it was a once in a lifetime holiday. After several failed attempts to persuade them, they finally caved in and agreed but with the proviso that my brother joined me on the holiday. Peter my elder brother was in his final year at school and I'm still not sure if he was a willing volunteer or just got fed up of me trying to persuade him to join me as from my mother point of view, his involvement was essential if I was to go. In the end, my scheming eventually paid off and on Saturday 22nd August 1964, my parents were driving the two of us into Manchester for a 09.30 departure from Manchester Victoria to Glasgow Central station.

I can't remember the exact number of pupils from school who booked on the holiday but it must have been at least thirty. By this time the Glasgow service had been taken over by English Electric Type 4 diesels, previously it would have been a Britannia, Jubilee or Royal Scot but not to worry too much, I was off to Scotland. After quickly noting down any engines at Victoria station we were soon on our way with D287 doing the hard work up front. The service was routed via Bolton, Preston, Lancaster, Carlisle and finally arriving at Glasgow early afternoon. The journey up to Glasgow proved interesting as a lot of my friends didn't realise, I had such an interest in trains, this also surprised some of the teaching staff who were our escorts during the entire holiday. I was kept extremely busy on the journey up to Carlisle, where we started to see some more interesting locomotives, none more so than the sight of 46200 'Princess Royal' stored out of use on the right-hand side as we passed Carlisle Upperby shed. It had been withdrawn about two years earlier but think it had been retained just in case Billy Butlin decided to buy it for display at one of his Holiday Camp Sites. He had already bought a number of other Stanier Pacific's from British Railways and it was hoped that 'Princess Royal' would be another of his acquisitions. Unfortunately, this wasn't to be the case and this splendid locomotive made its final journey a month later to Coatbridge near Glasgow for scrapping. Once we had departed Carlisle, virtually every locomotive I saw was Scottish based, so completely new to me, the equivalent of being from a different world, well we were in Scotland! On arrival at Glasgow Central station, we were greeted with the magnificent sight of Duchess Pacific 46244 'Kings George VI', which had earlier arrived with a special summer holiday service from Blackpool and was still resting at the buffer stops at Central station. I took a photograph of the Duchess which proved a complete waste of time and film as my Kodak Brownie just couldn't handle the light conditions inside the station building, resulting in a dark image with little clue an engine was somewhere on the photograph. When we eventually found the platform for a train to Wemyss Bay, another school from Knutsford had joined our group, unfortunately the authorities at Central station hadn't increased the size of the train, resulting in all of us being squeezed in to two coaches. The train was so full that some of the small boys were forced on to the upper luggage racks. Thankfully, I wasn't one of the unlucky individuals and I somehow managed to get a seat on the right-hand side next to a window. At least I had the benefit of the service being steam hauled by a British Railways Standard tank engine: 80108. This was before the new blue electric EMU's took over most of the suburban services out of Glasgow Central station, with the line to Wemyss Bay eventually being electrified during 1967. Finally, we arrived at the fabulous terminus station at Wemyss Bay. The station building dates back to 1903 and was originally built by the Caledonian Railways and made considerable use of glass held in place by a curved steel structure. The station also had the benefit of being directly connected to the adjoining ferry terminal for services to the Isle of Bute. Consequently, after a short walk across to the quayside where the historic paddle steamer 'The Waverley' awaited us. The ferry dates back to 1946 and was a fitting means of transport for our journey across to the Isle of Bute. We were staying at a camp site close to Rothesay and we made the final part of our journey in a number of coaches.

I was invited to share a chalet with a classroom colleague Kevin Farrell, who I'd had little to do with prior to holiday. The holiday involved numerous day trips to various locations across the west coast of Scotland, including a day trip on a ferry further down the coast to Largs, which again had a fabulous station terminus which I visited during our time there. The highlight of the trip being a ferry across to the mainland then a coach journey to the Nuclear submarine base at Faslane. Most evenings the camp site provided entertainment in large wooden hut when we were allowed a certain amount of freedom to enjoy the disco or other entertainment. Two of the big hits at the time, included Manfred Mans: 5-4-3-2-1 and Do Wah Diddy Diddy with Paul Jones providing the vocals on both tracks. The reason I mention Paul Jones, is that until 2018 he hosted the Blues Show on Radio 2, which was about the only radio programme I made the effort to listen to in recent years.

I must admit it was an enjoyable holiday other than one member of staff who had a bad track record of dishing out punishment to pupils whether they deserved it or not. During one of our meals, which involved eating fish he decided I should eat the whole of my fish which at the time I found revolting and sometimes would make me physically sick. So as punishment, he threatened to cane me until one of the more caring members of staff intervened and stopped him carrying out his punishment, which I'm sure this particular member of staff got great pleasure from. Thankfully, since my late teens, my tastes have changed and I now really enjoy eating fish.

After all the excitement of the holiday, the day of our return soon arrived and on Saturday 29th August 1964, we were on the Paddle Steamer 'Waverley' for our return journey back across to the mainland at Wemyss Bay. This time the size of the train had been increased, so there was space for all of us to sit down and once again a British Railways Standard tank: 80116 hauled us back to Glasgow Central station. Here we were booked to travel on the 09.30 service back to Manchester Victoria with English Electric Type 4 diesel D255 doing the honours. The return south again provided plenty of opportunity for noting down more Scottish based locomotives on the journey down to Carlisle, including a pair of Scottish based LNER V2's: 60931 and 60957, soon followed by 60818. These were the first Gresley V2's I had ever seen, so a very memorable occasion. At Carlisle two of the remaining LMS Royal Scots were noted i.e. 46132 'The King's Regiment Liverpool' and 46160 'Queen Victoria's Rifleman' plus my final two Duchess's of the trip: 46255 'City of Hereford', which only had a few weeks remaining in service before being hauled across to its final resting place at Arnott Young scrapyard in Troon, Scotland and 46243 'City of Lancaster' which again was withdrawn by October 1964 and hauled to the Central Wagon scrapyard, Ince, Wigan for scrapping, a sad end for two magnificent locomotives. We finally arrived safely back at Manchester Victoria station where my parents were waiting to take us home.

Here the teacher who saved me from being caned, asked my parents if; Ian found fish difficult to eat, to which my Mum confirmed she never gave me fish at meal times as it made him physically ill. No doubt he made sure that his colleague knew this fact! I wouldn't have been surprised if both my parents were convinced that both of us had enjoyed the holiday, although to be honest it wasn't too difficult to understand that it wasn't my brothers Peters idea of a perfect holiday.

Manchester and local North West Sheds

As an alternative to our usual visits to Stockport Edgeley and Heaton Mersey sheds on most Saturdays, we made the decision to venture into Manchester for our first visit on the 7th November 1964 with the aim of visiting Newton Heath shed which had the shed code of 9D. I met Michael at Manchester Piccadilly station followed by a brisk walk over to Manchester Victoria station, which I had only once before visited during my school trip to Scotland. From Manchester Victoria station we took a local service to Dean Lane station, which was located virtually next to the shed at Newton Heath. We had no problems gaining access to the shed and we were soon in to our stride and found the shed fairly full of locomotives including one Britannia 70049 'Solway Firth' a Carlisle based engine, which had obviously made its way down to Manchester on one of the services from north of the border. The shed was fairly large and housed six LMS Jubilee's three operational: 45580 'Burma' a recent transfer from Warrington Dallam shed, 45642 'Boscowen' a Newton Heath engine for most of its life and 45653 'Barham' a recent arrival from Blackpool. Then a further three Jubilee's were on the scrap line: 45592 'Indore' a former Carnforth engine, 45601 'British Guiana' and 45623 'Palestine'. The depot at the time was still basically a steam shed with just a few diesels present. The range of steam locomotives on the depot covered a wide range of classes from the relatively small Jinty 0-6-0 shunting engines to the huge BR Standard built 2-10-0 9F's.

My second visit to Newton Heath took place on the 20th February 1965 and once again we met up at Manchester Piccadilly and made our way across to Victoria, where we noted Jubilee 45593 'Kholapur', which at the time had recently been transferred from Patricroft shed to Newton Heath, basically a move across Manchester for this locomotive. It was later transferred to Leeds Holbeck, where it joined fellow class members in the last stronghold of the class. Today, 'Kholapur' is now preserved at the railway museum at Tyseley with three other members of the class being preserved at different preservation sites. We were soon on our way to Dean Lane station and into the main shed building at Newton Heath. The alarming sight of two Jubilees on the scrap line that we had seen in steam during our previous visit just three months earlier: 45580 and 45642, more alarming was the fact that Britannia 70017 'Arrow' had joined them, more about this particular Britannia's later on.

Around this period, I must have become even more desperate to satisfy the need of my hobby as later in the day I visited my usual Saturday haunt at Stockport Edgeley and found two Jubilees on the depot: 45596 'Bahamas' and 45632 'Tonga'. I still had time for my usual walk down to Tiviot Dale station to view the departures for Derby and Sheffield, with LNER B1 61051 working on the Sheffield service but unfortunately Peak Diesel D141 on the Derby service. I was obviously set in my ways, as I travelled back to Woodley from Manchester on a local service then caught the bus to Stockport Edgeley as I would have done on a normal Saturday. Why I didn't catch a train direct from Piccadilly to Stockport then walk to the shed still puzzles me. But as a twelve-year-old you stuck with a routine that you felt safe with and didn't do anything that could potentially cause problems like jumping on the wrong train that didn't stop at Stockport Edgeley!

The next new shed to visit in the Manchester area was on Saturday 28th August 1966 at Trafford Park with the shed code of 9E. By this time the shed was still a hive of activity with just short of fifty locomotives on the shed that day. The bulk being steam, which also included twelve LMS designed tank engines, basically Fairburn and Stanier designs. These engines were still being used for empty coaching stock movements in and out of Manchester Central station. The station only had roughly 3 years before it was closed in May 1969 and finally in the early 1980's was transformed into the G-MEX exhibition centre. Today if you stand across from the entrance to the complex, it is still fairly obvious that the building was a former railway terminus with a single span roof.

On the same day I visited Reddish shed 9C and Longsight shed 9A for my first visit since our cycling adventure a year earlier. Reddish shed was modern purpose-built depot to service the EM1 and EM2 electric locomotives that operated on the 1500 DC electrified route via Woodhead to Sheffield. Whereas, Longsight was a former steam depot that had been adapted to provide servicing facilities for diesel and the new AC electric locomotives used on the electrified route to Crewe and eventually onto London Euston.

Then on the 8th October 1966 the time had arrived for a visit to Patricroft (9H) shed which would be the last steam depot in the Manchester area that we hadn't previously visited that was still operational. At the time we had both noticed that the Locomotive Club of Great Britain (LCGB) had been advertising the 'Crab Commemorative Railtour' which originated in Liverpool Exchange station and travelled east to Goole via Manchester Victoria. The Crab was the nickname given to a class of steam locomotives first introduced in 1926 and designed by the former Lancashire and Yorkshire Railways (L&YR) and London Midland and Scottish (LMS) Chief Mechanical Engineer George Hughes. The Crabs had been a very common sight in and around the Manchester area, especially Stockport and Gorton sheds which both had an allocation of Crabs during the time period covered by this book until their demise at the end of 1966. It was not unusual to find four or more examples of Crabs on Stockport Edgeley shed in the years leading up to 1966.

We headed over to Manchester Victoria after completing our respective paper rounds. By about 10.45 am, Crab 42942 arrived from Liverpool into Victoria station. Owing to the nine-coach load of the special, the decision was taken to attach a pilot engine in the shape of LMS Black 5: 45336 and soon the pair were heading east via Accrington, Sowerby Bridge, Wakefield and finally onto Goole. The Black 5 only acted as a pilot until Stansfield Hall after Rose Grove, where the Crab continued unassisted to Wakefield Kirkgate, where it was replaced by a War Department (WD) 90076 for the journey to Goole. The Crab made its own way across to Goole, to enable it to work the railtour back to Liverpool Exchange unassisted.

After taking a few photographs, it was time to watch the railtour depart Victoria station and a short walk to board a local stopping service to Patricroft station which was located on the west side of Manchester. The shed was a short five-minute walk from the station and involved a walk along footbridge that dropped you into the shed yard. The shed was formed of two dead end building in a 'L' shape with one shed having eight tracks and the other ten. This shed along with Newton Heath originally provided the bulk of the locomotives for services working from Manchester Victoria and Exchange stations. The depot comprised a sizeable allocation of British Railways Standard Class 5 steam locomotives, which were generally employed on services along the North Wales coast plus other duties like express parcel services. On the day of our visit twenty-eight examples were on the depot, this was in addition to the seven examples noted at Victoria station earlier in the day. Another reason for visiting the shed at Patricroft was their allocation of British Railways Standard built 3MT tank engines, original built at Swindon works and until their transfer to Patricroft a completely alien engine to us young spotters from Manchester. During our visit five of the class were eking out their existence at the shed. All five examples had recently been transferred from Machynlleth shed in mid Wales and only lasted just over a year at Patricroft before going for scrap. A large number of the class had been allocated to Western Region sheds with a substantial number allocated to the Southern Region shed at Nine Elms near London Waterloo, for working the empty coaching stock duties out of that London terminus.

A real surprise for us at Patricroft was the sight of a 47201, an engine dating back to 1899 which had spent most of its life since the early 1950's at various sheds in the North West. Finally arriving at Patricroft around the time of our visit. It only lasted a few months before being sent for scrap at T Wards, Beighton, Sheffield. After our visit, we headed back to Manchester Piccadilly via Victoria station. At Piccadilly station we noted a Stratford allocated Type 3 diesel: D6713 working the 14.37 boat service to Harwich, which incidentally at the time stopped at Guide Bridge, an unknown fact to us youngster, otherwIse we could have travelled on it to Guide Bridge, instead of the local DMU. Although at the time this was virtually a daily service, the sight of a Type 3 diesel from Stratford, London, was still a relatively rare sight and was one of the reasons why myself and Michael regularly visited Newton station to watch it either heading into Manchester Piccadilly or its return east towards Harwich.

One last memory I have of our trips into Manchester, was on Saturday 23rd April 1966, when the Altrinchamian Railway Excursion Society ran the 'Waverley Special' from Manchester Exchange to Edinburgh Waverley using a number of steam locomotives but more importantly a very rare LNER Class A2: 60528 'Tudor Minstrel' on the departure leg of the special out of Manchester Exchange station. This was the societies first railtour and boy would I have loved to have travelled on it but the cost would have been just too expensive for both of us. However, the plan was to watch it depart Exchange station, as usual I had arranged to meet Michael at Piccadilly station then walk across to Exchange station, unfortunately, during my paper round, I somehow managed to crash my bike, resulting in the front wheel becoming buckled. With a never give up attitude I carried my bike and completed the paper round before arriving late back home and missing the planned train service into Piccadilly. My Dad was very concerned that I had hurt myself but I just pressed on and caught the next service into Manchester, where Michael was still waiting for me. The delay made it virtually impossible to see the departure of the special but we did our best and arrived at Exchange station as the special was just disappearing around the curve towards Salford Central station only to see the smoke rising above the building in the foreground and the last few coaches disappearing around the bend. If I'd had access to mobile phones back then, I would have called Michael and told him to make his own way across Exchange station, sadly it wasn't the case and Michael showed his true loyalty by waiting, resulting in both of us missing the special.

We didn't let the upset of missing the 'Tudor Minstrel', depress us too much and decided to visit Newton Heath shed, which I suspect we would have originally done. We were both pleased to find Britannia 70000, itself present on the shed that day and a took a photograph of it in the shed yard on my relatively new Kodak Instamatic camera. Amazingly, owing to the good weather conditions, I somehow managed to produce a half decent photograph, which was also the case with the photograph I took of Stanier tank engine 42548 whilst it was on the shed turntable. In those days you would have to wait sometime for the film to be processed and then collect the prints and negatives from the Chemist, which was one of the few options you had to develop and print a film. This was in the days before companies like Bonusprint appeared, who specialised in mail order film processing making themselves considerably cheaper than the local Chemist.

To have had the luxury of a Digital Camera or mobile phone with a decent built-in camera in those days would have been fantastic! Instant pictures as opposed to waiting until you finished the film then taking it to the Chemist.

70000 'Britannia on Newton Heath shed - 23rd April 1966

42548 on the turntable at Newton Heath shed - 23rd April 1966

Needless to say, my run of good luck of taking half decent photographs ended when I took a photograph of Jinty locomotive 47383, which I must have rushed as I missed part of the smoke box! I would later see the same Jinty at Westhouses shed during January 1968. This engine was eventually saved by a bunch of enthusiasts and is now based on the Severn Valley Railway, although not currently in working order. Finally, Britannia was joined by three fellow class members at Newton Heath shed that day: 70017 'Arrow', 70021 'Morning Star' and 70044 'Earl Haig', I had earlier seen 70015 'Apollo' when I passed through Guide Bridge.

Saturday 2nd December 1967, we decided to visit two new sheds relatively local to us in the North West: Bolton shed (9K) and Wigan Springs Branch shed (8F). As this was a local trip, we both completed our paper rounds then met up as usual at Manchester Piccadilly station prior to arriving at Victoria station for our local service to Bolton. We passed Bolton shed on our left as we approached Bolton station, which helped with locating it later. After about a fifteen-minute walk we had reached the shed and quickly started our tour of the shed noting about twenty steam locomotives on the shed, with half being withdrawn these included a number of BR Standard Class 5's: 73004, 73014, 73048 and 73156. However, 73069 was still operational and was seen passing the shed light engine. This engine was used on a series of railtours during 1968 as I believe it became the last none Caprotti Vale Gear example in service.

The Caprotti Valve Gear was a type of valve gear used on steam locomotives in place of the standard piston valves and was invented by an Italian engineer Arturo Caprotti. During the 1950's this form of valve gear was improved and incorporated in a number of locomotive designs at the time including a number of Stanier Black 5's and thirty BR Standard Class 5's and also the famous and unique locomotive BR Standard Class 8 71000 'Duke of Gloucester'. The Black 5's and the Duke had been withdrawn well before the final year of steam. However, many of the BR Standard Class 5's were still in daily use operating from Patricroft.

From Bolton we took a local service to Wigan Wallgate and used our Shed Directory to locate the shed known as Springs Branch. The shed would close to steam operation just two days later, so by the time we had arrived it was virtually a diesel depot. Only five steam locomotives were noted in steam during our visit with only 48292 being on the shed, whilst 44831, 48620, 48665 and 48764 were seen working in and around the shed. We caught a direct service back to Manchester Victoria station and noted 73125 passing light engine through the station, whilst Britannia Pacific 70012 'John of Gaunt' arrived with a parcel service.

The final shed we visited that could be classified as local was at Buxton (9L) when we used a Manchester Piccadilly to Buxton service from Stockport to reach the shed. This was on the 9th December 1967 and clearly indicated that we were determined to visit as many of the remaining sheds before the end of steam operation. Steam would finally come to an end at Buxton on the 4th March 1968, so was still active during our visit, with six Stanier 8F's on the shed and four being in steam, whilst 4 Stanier 8F's were withdrawn and positioned alongside the shed. This was my first visit to Buxton shed since the Buckley Wells coach tour back in May 1965 and it was immediately obvious that the shed was being run down ready for its closure. Most of the work at the shed was a result of the heavy freight trains originating from the quarries located nearby at Peak Forest. After closure of the steam shed, a new diesel depot opened close to the town's railway station to provide covered servicing and fuelling facilities for the diesels that had replaced the Stanier 8F's.

After arriving back in Stockport, we couldn't resist a quick visit to Edgeley shed which had thirteen active steam on hand that day.

Leeds and York Trips

By February 1965, we had identified Leeds as a possible place of interest, which was helped when we discovered that Stalybridge station had a regular service to Leeds and with some of these services heading further north on to Newcastle. Stalybridge was relatively easy to reach as a regular bus service operated from Hyde. However, if we had known a rail service operated between Stockport and Stalybridge, which stopped at Guide Bridge station we would have almost certainly have used that as an alternative to the bus, the ignorance of youth!

On Saturday 13th February 1965, we boarded our train at Stalybridge en-route to Yorkshire. I can clearly recall the excitement on the journey east as the first part of the line ran parallel with a freight line known as the Micklehurst Loop. This route had been added around 1885 to prevent freight trains from causing delays for the faster passenger services. During the journey to Huddersfield, we noted a number of heavy freights heading east with a WD and a BR Standard built 9F working hard on the climb over the Pennines. Before reaching Leeds, our train passed sheds at Huddersfield (55G), Mirfield (56D) and Farnley Junction (55C), so even more activity as we regularly leaned out of the windows in an attempt to note down any engines that were visible on the sheds that we passed.

Our arrival at Leeds City station coincided with the departure of Jubilee 45647 'Sturdee' on a passenger service I suspect to Carlisle via the Settle and Carlisle route. At this time, Leeds had two stations, Central and City, which were virtually joined together and now form one station known as Leeds City railway station. A quick visit into Central station enabled us to see our first Deltic diesel locomotive: D9017 'The Durham Light Infantry', these English Electric built diesel locomotives were at the time the most powerful diesels operating on the British rail network. The power was provided via two 18-cylinder Napier engines, originally designed for operation in a marine environment. The two power units delivered a massive 3,300 BHP and 50,000 lbs of Tractive Effort, which at the time was very impressive. Twenty-two locomotives were built and delivered from 1961 and effectively replaced a much larger fleet of Gresley design Class A3 and A4 Pacific steam locomotives. I was hoping that some of the Gresley Pacific's would still be in operation on the Leeds to London Kings Cross route, but unfortunately, we were too late by a year or two.

After the visit to Central station, we used our Ian Allan Shed Directory to find Leeds Holbeck shed (55A), which at the time was the main depot in the Leeds operational area and was still a very busy steam shed. The shed comprised two brick-built roundhouses, linked together providing cover for a large number of locomotives. In addition, the shed had a huge coaling plant plus staff offices and engineering facilities for the repair of the locomotives and a relatively new diesel servicing depot. The shed at Holbeck became a mecca for railway photography, owing to the roof lighting combined with the atmosphere created by steam rising from the locomotives which produced a very evocative scene for photographing steam locomotives in their declining years.

At the time of our visit there were almost forty locomotives on the depot ranging from LMS types: Black 5's, 8F's and Jubilees plus a range of LMS designed tank engines and a number of LNER B1's. In addition, the shed contained Royal Scot Class: 46160 'Queen Victoria's Rifleman' and one of the last four remaining Patriot Class: 45512 'Bunsen'. Unfortunately, the Type 4 Peak diesels were well in evidence after taking over many of passenger routes operating around Leeds. As mentioned earlier, Holbeck shed became the final strong hold for the LMS Jubilees and during our visit the following were present: 45602 'British Honduras', 45608 'Gibraltar', 45626 'Seychelles', 45658 'Keyes', 45661 'Vernon' and 45697 'Achilles'. Strangely, no sign of the most infamous Jubilee allocated to Holbeck: 45562 'Alberta', which lasted to the end of steam in Yorkshire on the 4th November 1967. Alberta was one of the last remaining Jubilees that managed to make it into 1967, with all of them allocated to Holbeck shed. Many enthusiasts expected 'Alberta' to be preserved but towards the end of its long career it had developed a number of mechanical problems. The decision was taken to save 45593 'Kholapur', resulting in 'Alberta' going for scrap at Cashmore's, Great Bridge, an undignified end for such a highly regarded locomotive. Apparently, someone managed to acquire the chimney from Alberta, so it's not been completely erased from history! As an indication, of how popular 'Alberta' was, the West Coast Railways at Carnforth who own two active Jubilees, recently changed the identity of one of their Jubilees: 45699 'Galatea' to that of 45562 'Alberta', which is now resplendent with a fresh coat of BR Brunswick green paint and new numbers and nameplate. The change of identity of 'Alberta' isn't permanent and as usual the change has either been supported by enthusiasts or caused a level of unrest with those who don't believe that a locomotives identity should ever be changed.

Leeds fast became one of our more popular destinations and each visit increased the number of sheds we would visit in the area. Within about six weeks of our first visit, I had decided to return on my own and would visit: Leeds Holbeck (55A), Farnley Junction (55C), Stourton (55B) and Leeds Neville Hill (55H) sheds all in one visit. This time Holbeck housed almost fifty locomotives including one of the final Royal Scots in service: 46128 'The Lovat Scouts', (The Scot only survived for a further five weeks) and Britannia 70008 'Black Prince' plus a couple of LNER B1's 61196 and 61214 and the usual collection of Jubilee's.

Next shed on the agenda was Farnley Junction (55C), which only had ten locomotives present on that day but included my first Peppercorn designed LNER A1: 60131 'Osprey', which was visiting from its new home at Leeds Neville Hill. Three Jubilees were present including my local celebrity engine 45596 'Bahamas' allocated to Stockport Edgeley shed.

After I travelled down to Stourton shed (55B) which housed around twenty locomotives including a very special 8F: 48297. Whilst I was walking around the shed, I struck up a conversation with the driver of the 8F, who invited me into the cab of the locomotive. At the time this was one of those little pleasures that many young enthusiasts just couldn't resist. Once in the cab he surprisingly asked if I fancied the challenge of driving the engine out of the shed into the shed yard, my jaw must have dropped to floor with the utter surprise as a result of his kind offer. There was no funny business as the driver was obviously a genuinely nice bloke and obviously had the time and patience. After a short set of instructions, I placed the 8F in to forward gear, released the train brake then forced the regulator handle up, which supplied the steam to the cylinders and off we went in the direction of the shed yard. I then engaged the train brake and we came to a halt after a run of about 200 yds. Not surprisingly, I doubt I'd ever been so excited in my young life and truly thanked the driver for his generosity and kindness. It's a pity he didn't need to drive the engine to Leeds, as I'm sure he would have given me a lift but he was off to collect a freight from one of the local freight yards.

The kindness of that driver was not uncommon around that time and many drivers appreciated the enthusiasm that the young kids at that time had for the railways. That attitude has somewhat changed with time and unfortunately not for the better.

After I arrived back in Leeds, I headed across to Neville Hill shed which was alongside the main line from Leeds to York. The shed had been under the management control of the York area but following a relatively recent reorganisation, found itself under control of Leeds. The shed had a small steam allocation and only had 13 locomotives present that day. However, this included another two LNER A1's: 60118 'Archibald Sturrock' and 60134 'Foxhunter' plus three Raven designed Q6's that originally dated back to 1913: 63344, 63417 and 63426, these were a North Eastern Railways design and a completely new class for me. The last locomotives of any note were two recently preserved engines LNER N7 tank engine 69621 dating back to 1924 and Gresley Class K4: 61994 (alternatively numbered 3442) 'The Great Marquess' an engine that had spent most of its working life in Scotland and was originally purchased from British Railways by Viscount Garnock but is now owned by John Cameron i.e., the legendary owner of Gresley Class A4: 60009 'Union of South Africa'.

After Neville Hill I made a quick return to Leeds, first popping into Central station to see the first member of the Deltic diesel class D9000 'Royal Scots Grey' ready to depart with the 16.40 Leeds to London Kings Cross - The White Rose. Then it was time to return to Stalybridge noting named LNER B1 61017 'Bushbuck' and BR Standard 9F, 92239 which was by now a York based engine, both on Mirfield shed. A truly unforgettable trip with Leeds fast becoming one of my favourite destinations.

By the end of 1965 I had worked out a plan to visit Doncaster via Leeds. This would be my first visit to Doncaster but unfortunately it was after all the former Eastern Region Pacific's had made their final journey to the scrapyards. The only part of the plan I hadn't been able to work out was the part of the journey from Leeds to Doncaster and by the time I had got to Leeds Central station the only option to get to Doncaster that morning was on a Pullman Service (I Suspect the Yorkshire Pullman) heading to London Kings Cross. This would have involved an extra payment of two shillings and sixpence for the privilege of travelling on a Pullman train. Although that was a considerable sum of money, remembering I was only paid 15 shillings for my weekly paper round, it had to be done. I remember sitting at my table (including curtains and a fancy lamp) with a very posh elderly lady sitting opposite. I can remember the puzzled look on her face as this young scruffy boy had the nerve to sit opposite her but this was the seat assigned to me on my Pullman service ticket. I think she thought I would be ejected by the coach attendant, when he came around to check tickets but I was travelling legitimately, so she had to put up with me all the way to Doncaster. Needless to say, I was more concerned that I didn't miss any engines and was busy recording everything we passed in my small notebook. However, I did record a LNER O4: 63765 but later discovered that this locomotive had been withdrawn in 1964, so I had obviously recorded the wrong number. Since then, with some research, there is a strong possibility that it was more than likely 63785, which was a Doncaster based O4 and survived until the end of March 1966. This class of locomotive dated back to 1911 and was designed by John G. Robinson the Chief Mechanical Engineer for the former Great Central Railway in the early part of the 20th century. These 2-8-0 locomotives were extensively used on coal trains in this part of the Eastern Region plus the North Midlands.

After a short time on the station at Doncaster I headed off to the shed using my trusted Shed Directory for guidance. The shed still had a significant number of steam engines present but Brush Type 4's and English Electric Type 3's were fast becoming the norm. The first port of call was the scrap line that contained eleven steam engines which I tried to photograph with my new Kodak Instamatic Camera bought with the Christmas tips I received from my paper round. Unfortunately, the foggy damp dark conditions at the time weren't conducive to taking photographs on a simple camera like the Instamatic and resulted in all the photos being very poor in quality.

The shed did however contain plenty of Eastern Region O4's, WD's and BR Standard 9F's plus a number of B1's, so well worth the effort. After the visit to the shed, I returned to the station and spent a few hours there noting a mixture of steam and diesel; including Gresley Pacific A3 60103 'Flying Scotsman' which passed through hauling a rake of coaches. By the time I started my return home it was just too dark to be able to identify anything, so a very uneventful return back to Stalybridge.

My first trip to York, was on the 11th December 1965. The day started well with the sight of Britannia 70026 'Polar Star' at Stalybridge on a parcels service. The usual route to Leeds and time for a quick visit to Leeds Holbeck before heading off to York. I'm glad I made the effort to get to Holbeck shed that day as I was stunned to see Battle of Britain Class: 34051 'Winston Churchill' on shed along with former Southern Region BR Standard Class 5: 73112 'Morgan Le Fay'. The Battle of Britain was on route to Hellifield for storage, whilst the Standard was on route for scrapping at T Wards, Beighton, Sheffield. I suspect the Standard had been used to haul the Battle of Britain up from the Southern Region to Holbeck but I've not seen anything to confirm this. Hellifield was at the time being used to store locomotives that were part of the National Collection prior to the conversion of York shed into the National Railway Museum and presumably the authorities thought the locomotives would be safe in such a remote place.

After leaving Leeds for York, we passed Class Q6: 63387 hauling a BR diesel shunter towards York. At York, I was surprised to see a former North Eastern Railways (NER) J27 65823 dating back to 1908, carryout some shunting duties close to the station. Also, at York was one of the elusive Tyne Dock allocated 9F's 92093, at that time as far as I was concerned the North East based 9F's might as well been based on the other side of the planet.

The line of withdrawn engines on York Shed contained some surprises, the first that a Peppercorn A1 had made it to December 1965, as 60151

'Midlothian' was joined by the following withdrawn locomotives: 60810, 60876, 60877, 61018, 61049, 61176, 61256, 61275, 62010, 65844, 65846, 65894 and 90045. The shed still contained plenty of former Eastern Region engines, including K1's, B1's and WD's plus three operational V2's: 60831, 60837 and 60886.

With regard to the A1 Pacific's, 60145 'St Mungo' was the last operational A1, surviving until June 1966 and later hauled to Hull Dairycoates shed for scrapping at the nearby Drapers scrapyard. This was the last member of the class, so the class had effectively become extinct, until a group of likeminded enthusiasts formed the 'A1 Steam Locomotive Trust' back in 1990 with the objective of building a new A1 Pacific from scratch. Nothing like this had ever been done before in Britain and many thought the group to be just a bunch of over excited men wanting to achieve an impossible dream. Originally 49 Peppercorn A1's had been built at Doncaster and were considered by many to be one of the best engineered Pacific's to work on the East Coast Main Line (ECML). On the 29th July 2008, their dreams of building the 50th A1 Pacific had come to fruition and 60163 'Tornado' moved under its own power. Soon after, it was transported to the Great Central Railway (GCR) where it was gradually run in and achieved speeds of sixty miles an hour, with the view that it would operate on the national network at speeds up to ninety miles an hour. During 2017, Network Rail allowed 'Tornado' to run at a speed of 100 mph during a test on the line between Darlington and York and 'Yes' it did achieve that incredible milestone and also made it onto that evenings National BBC News.

New build A1 Pacific 60163 'Tornado' at Manchester Piccadilly station Prior to working the 'The Bard of Avon' railtour to Strafford on Avon

After the visit to the shed I found time to visit the former railway museum at York, before the current National Railway Museum moved into the former York shed. At the time there were 10 locomotives on display at the old museum, a far cry from that of today's National Railway Museum. The journey back to Stalybridge proved fairly uneventful but for a change I travelled on a loco hauled service with Peak diesel D187 doing the honours. This made a change from the usual diesel multiple units that I had previous travelled on to and from Stalybridge.

By October 1966, I had organised a second trip to York on Saturday 22nd October. The date determined by the fact that a railtour had been advertised to run that day, from London Kings Cross to Newcastle, using 60103 'Flying Scotsman' and more interestingly Southern Region Merchant Navy 35026 'Lamport and Holt Line'. The railtour was called 'The Elizabethan Railtour'. The original railtour was advertised with both an A4 and an A2 class locomotive, but unfortunately both the intended locomotives were withdrawn from service prior to the running of the railtour, so Scotsman and the Merchant Navy were late substitutions. This time my trusty Kodak Instamatic actually managed to take some recognisable photographs of the Merchant Navy at York station plus one of 'Flying Scotsman' on York shed after arriving with the railtour from London.

Merchant Navy 35026 'Lamport & Holt Line'
York station 22nd October 1966

After the excitement of watching the railtour arrive and depart, I was off to York Shed (50A), no need for the Shed directory as the depot was visible from York station and indeed just a ten-minute walk. Although there was still an impressive display of steam engines on the shed, it was just a shadow of its former self, as diesels had certainly blitzed steam from virtually all passenger services on the East Coast Main Line. One of the last operational LNER V2's 60831 was in steam inside the shed, whilst fellow class member 60806 was dumped outside in the shed yard. Inside the shed was Gresley Pacific A4 60019 'Bittern' which was still in service and subsequently used on the RCTS

'The Waverley' railtour on the 12th November 1966. The tour originated from York and involved an out and back to Edinburgh Waverley station. I just wish I had made the effort to get to York much earlier than I did, as I missed all the Peppercorn A1's that York had become famous for, although there were still a small batch of LNER K1's working off the shed, so not a complete waste of a visit.

LNER A3 4472 'Flying Scotsman' being serviced on York shed
After arriving with the special from Kings Cross 22nd October 1966

My final visit to York during the 1960's was on the 29th July 1967 with steam just clinging on at Leeds Holbeck shed but steam had virtually been eliminated at York, other than a couple of Gresley Class A4's: 60007 'Sir Nigel Gresley' and 60019 'Bittern' both had been privately purchased and I suspect were waiting to find new homes. 60007 was later sent to Crewe Works during August 1967, where parts from 60026 were used to restore 60007.

As mentioned earlier in this chapter, Drapers scrapyard at Hull accounted for over 700 locomotives being scrapped during the 1960's. Many of the engines arriving from sheds within the Eastern Region of British Railways e.g., York, Wakefield and Hull Dairycoates etc. However, Albert Draper the owner of the scrap merchant's business decided one of the last steam locomotives to arrive for scrapping a Stanier Black 5: 45305 would be saved and he paid for its full restoration and handed over the locomotive to the 'Humberside Locomotive Preservation Group' for them to maintain the locomotive. The engine is still owned by the Draper family but is now under the care of the 5305 Locomotive Association, the successor to the previous group given charge to maintain the engine and is usually found at the preserved railway known as the Great Central Railway.

Stanier Black 5: 45305 at the Great Central Railway
12th February 2011

Trainspotting Clubs and Societies

In the late 1950's and early 1960's trainspotting had become hugely popular, so much so that many schools had their own clubs to support those interested in railways. Alternatively, many societies sprung up across the country offering organised trips to sheds and railway workshops up and down the country. You usually had to become a member before you could take advantage of any of the organised events. In addition, other benefits including receipt of the society magazine, reporting the latest news of locomotive withdrawals and transfers plus details of scheduled shed visits etc. During the early part of 1964, I joined one of the local societies called 'The Buckley Wells Railway Enthusiasts' who at the time were based in Bury, north Manchester. The society operated regular coach tours to destinations all over the country. Most coach tours would be a single day but the more complex trips usually involved an overnight or in some cases a full weekend. The society later became the 'Buckley Wells Transport Society'.

A copy of Magazine No 11 after the society had changed its name.
This magazine covered the period January to March 1968

After becoming a member and receiving my first society magazine, I noticed they intended to run a North Midlands coach tour on Saturday 22nd May 1965. With convenient coach pickups at Manchester and Stockport, all for

£1.00. The tour was scheduled to visit ten sheds in the North Midlands plus Derby Works, so I took the plunge and sent off my booking form along with a £1.00 postal order. Postal orders were the method that individuals paid for things in those days, as a twelve-year-old certainly wouldn't have had access to a bank account and cheque book facilities. I seem to recall I went on this tour on my own and possibly caught a bus into Stockport to meet the coach. This was a real adventure and opened up a whole new world for me, as I had never been on such a well organised and complex event like this before.

On the day I caught the usual bus into Stockport and waited for the coach to arrive at the front of Stockport Town Hall. The coach arrived on time at 08.30 and off we went heading east towards Derby travelling via Ashbourne and eventually arrived at the main entrance to Derby Works and after a short delay off we went in to the works visiting many large buildings that were being used to maintain various classes of diesel locomotives. At the time Derby Works was building a new batch of Type 2 diesels, many of which were being used in the Derby and Nottingham area. Only one steam engine was present inside the works: 90381 but this changed as we walked over to the shed at Derby. Prior to that we had seen eleven Type 2 diesels under construction but more importantly we had seen four of the original diesel's locomotives built in the late 1940's and 1950's 10000, 10201, 10202 and 10203. I just wish I'd taken a camera, as this would be the only chance I would have to see these classic early diesel locomotives but the reality was I had broken my camera and couldn't afford to replace it.

The shed at Derby was immediately alongside the works and comprised a brick-built roundhouse and adjoining sidings. Inside the shed was one of the saddle tanks that worked the Cromford and High Peak Railway: 47000. Next stop was the huge new diesel depot at Toton along with the former steam shed. To be honest the diesel depot was just a case of noting down the numbers but it housed about sixty diesels: Peaks including D1, D2 and D10, Type 2's, Brush Type 4's and plenty of Diesel shunters. The steam shed was in its final days and housed just ten steam locomotives virtually all-in store but a number of operational steam locomotives were noted working in the yards across from the steam shed.

The next shed to visit was that at Nottingham classified as 16D at the time and had only recently closed as an operational steam depot on the 4th April 1965 and was now basically a diesel stabling point. However, steam refused to be erased from the depot and a single LMS Jinty was found inside the shed roundhouse: 47645 stored out of use and surrounded by diesels mainly recently built Type 2 diesels. The Jinty stay at Nottingham didn't last too long before it was hauled north to the scrapyard at Wards, Killamarsh, Sheffield during August 1965.

47645 withdrawn at Nottingham shed

After the less interesting visits to Toton and Nottingham, the coach then visited a further eight sheds only one being a diesel depot the rest were very much active steam sheds. The next shed on the tour was the impressive Colwick shed coded 40E and housing more than seventy locomotives, many had Eastern Region origins: B1's, O4's, WD's and a single K3: 61943 which was acting a stationary boiler within the main shed building. This was only the second member of the Gresley K3 class I had seen, the other one being the one I had earlier reported during my trip to Sheffield. I have recently discovered a photograph of 61943 outside Doncaster works in ex works condition during July 1961. So, after receiving a major works overall, less than 4 years later it was being used as a stationary steam boiler. Colwick shed was a huge 18 track dead end shed with its origins dating back to 1858 and formally a Great Northern Railway shed. It was a very impressive shed with the vast majority of the locomotives on shed that day unseen by myself before this visit. Other than two visiting 8F: 48551 from Crewe South shed, which eventually was transferred to my local shed at Heaton Mersey before its closure and 48305 another Crewe South engine and one that made it into preservation and is now based on the Great Central Railway (GCR) at Loughborough.

The next shed was Annesley coded 16B and alongside the former GCR line and home to many freight engines included eighteen British Railways Standard 9F's and dozens of Stanier Black 5's and 8F's. However, two Eastern Region engines were present that day, LNER V2 60828 and fellow LNER B1 61223. The shed was relatively small, having just 6 tracks housed in a brick building dating back to the days of the GCR. Its importance increased around 1963 when it received a batch of LMS Royal Scots for working the express services along the GCR, however, this didn't last long and just over a year later the Scots had all gone. By January 1966 the shed had closed with the rapid run down of the GCR with the eventual aim to close the entire route by the end of the 1960's. Thankfully, a part of the GCR survives today as the well-known preserved railway with the same name and the plan is to join up the southern part to the northern part to form a sizeable preserved railway.

Next on the schedule was Kirkby in Ashfield shed (16E) which was a relatively small shed with just a three-track brick-built building with an adjoining two track building of Midland Region origins. The shed closed to steam during October 1966 and at the time of my visit housed mainly Stanier 8F freight engines plus eight of Fowler designed 0-6-0 4F Midland freight engines. The writing was already on the wall with the presence of eight modern brush Type 4 diesels.

Westhouses shed 16G was next up with six tracks housed within a single brick built dead end shed of Midland Railway design. Like Kirkby in Ashfield, Westhouses housed a large number of Stanier 8F's and Fowler 0-6-0 4F's, with seven 4F's assigned to the scrap line. The shed was located very close to a Colliery and basically provided the engines for the freight that originated from the pit, including the supply of some Jinty 0-6-0 shunting engines, two were present during our visit: 47442 and 47543. A couple of Jinty's managed to cling on at Westhouses shed until January 1968, well after the end of steam in the Midlands and one of these 47383 made it into the preservation era on the Severn Valley Railway. The nearby Williamthorpe Colliery closed during August 1967, so the work for these small tank engines came to an end. I have a painting of 47383 during its final days at the colliery painted by Derbyshire born railway artists Colin Wright on my dining room wall. The depot continued with BR Class 20's diesel's replacing the steam locomotives but even their stay came to an end and the depot closed completely by 1987 and has since been completely erased with very little evidence that a depot ever existed.

Whilst on route to the two steam sheds at Staveley: Great Central shed and Barrow Hill shed, we stopped off at the recently opened diesel depot at Shirebrook, which only contained seven diesel engines. Next was the steam shed at Langwith Junction (41J) a small shed with a three-track brick-built shed adjoined to a two through track brick-built building. The shed was of GCR origins but closed during February 1966 with Shirebrook diesel depot taking over its responsibilities. At the time of our visit the shed still had a large number of Eastern based locomotives including: Robinson designed O4's, WD's and BR Standard 9F's. In addition, a few diesel shunters plus a single Clayton centre cab diesel which must have recently arrived from Staveley Barrow Hill shed.

The last two scheduled shed visits were Staveley Great Central and Barrow Hill sheds. The first being the Great Central shed (41H), with only a matter of weeks remaining before closure on the 20th June 1965. The locomotives present were very similar to that seen at Langwith Junction and eighteen engines on the shed plus another seven on the scrap line. The shed comprised five tracks with a dead end. Finally, we moved across to the shed known as Staveley Barrow Hill (41E), which is still standing today as Railway Heritage Centre and is I believe the only remaining former BR roundhouse still being used as it was originally intended, to house locomotives. At the time of our visit the shed still contained three of the tiny tank steam locomotives used at the nearby Staveley Works: 41533 a 0-4-0 tank engine dating back to 1907, 41835 0-6-0 tank engine design by Johnson to a Midland design and amazingly dating back to 1878 and finally 47001 a 0-4-0 saddle tank built by Kitson & Co at Hunslet, Leeds and dating back to 1932, so virtually still being run in when compared to its colleagues. We had earlier in the day seen 47000 on Derby shed. Apparently, an agreement had been signed in 1866 between the Midland Railway and Staveley Works that stipulated that the railway provide suitable motive power to operate the private railway within the works for 100 years. Because of the tight curves within the works, there was a need to maintain a small number of these tiny tank engines at Staveley Barrow Hill shed. The shed also contained ten Clayton Centre Cab diesels recently built at Beyer Peacock factory in Manchester, they didn't last long and were soon shipped off to Scotland to join their sisters north of the border. Problems with the class saw the first withdrawal taking place during July 1968 and by the end of 1971, all the class had been withdrawn with some members of the class only having a working life of five years. That apart, I will always remember my first visit to Barrow Hill shed for the sight of the diminutive tank engines.

After leaving Staveley, we should have headed directly back to Stockport and Manchester but the organisers were obviously in a good mood plus time must have been on our side, so we stopped off at the steam shed at Buxton (9L). This was my first visit to this Derbyshire shed, which still housed a number of former LNER J94 0-6-0ST saddle tanks, dating back to the early 1940's and based at Buxton to work the famous Cromford and High Peak Railway. In addition, the shed had Patriot 45522 'Prestatyn' which had been withdrawn during September 1964, so obviously the authorities had forgotten about it at this Derbyshire outpost. Finally, Jubilee 45705 'Seahorse' was on shed and still in operational use. This locomotive became famous for operating an express passenger service from Buxton to Manchester Central and return for the benefit of business men who required a quick service to the centre of Manchester, what a novel idea.

It was still light when we departed Buxton and on our way to the scheduled drop off points, mine being at Stockport Town Hall, then onto a bus back to Woodley and home. Before this coach tour of the North Midlands, I had never seen so many new locomotives, amazingly I recorded close to 500 new engines, which must have taken days to underline in my Ian Allan books.

My next trip with the Buckley Wells Railway Enthusiast was on Sunday 31st October 1965, which involved everyone meeting up at Manchester Piccadilly station by 08.30. Then catching the 08.50 service from Manchester Piccadilly to Wolverhampton for coach that toured sheds in the Wolverhampton and Birmingham area. The plan was to get up early have breakfast then walk from home to Bredbury station for local service to Manchester Piccadilly. Bredbury was the only station in the area that had a Sunday service that would deliver me to Piccadilly station by 08.30 am. My Dad got me up and made me breakfast and set me off on my way with a swift 30-minute walk to Bredbury station. Things didn't look good when I arrived at Bredbury station to find the main gate locked. In those days the station master lived in an adjoining house and must have heard me rattling the gate. After a short wait he arrived to unlock the gate and sold me my return ticket to Piccadilly station. Eventually the local stopping DMU arrived and off I went to Manchester. On arrival at Piccadilly, I was puzzled that nobody else was there, especially Michael. He eventually arrived and I asked him why he was late, to which he replied 'I'm not late' and followed by asking if I had forgotten to change my clock to take account of the one-hour time difference! Yes, I had obviously forgotten plus my Dad, what a clanger, no wonder the gates were locked at Bredbury station, I'd obviously caught the first service into Manchester and not the one I had planned to catch an hour later. Anyway, we were safely at Piccadilly station and were soon joined by other enthusiasts and some society officials. Then we all boarded the 08.50 departure and soon passing Edgeley shed which had Brit 70021 'Morning Star' visible, next point of interest was as we passed Stoke shed (5D) and somehow managed to record thirteen steam locomotives on the shed including three stored or withdrawn Jinty's: 47273, 47280 and 47307. At this time, Wolverhampton still had two stations, the current station which we arrived at plus the former GWR Low Level station which we saw Brush Type 4 D1751 departing on a passenger service.

After safely arriving at Wolverhampton, we were all marched off the station and boarded a locally hired coach for our first port of call Oxley shed (2B). Oxley was only a short distance from the station at Wolverhampton, so it didn't take too long to reach. This was the first time that either of us had been to Birmingham, so plenty of excitement. Oxley was a former GWR shed with a twin roundhouse and still housed twenty former GWR steam locomotives, however eleven of these were located on the scrap line. I was surprised to find five GWR Pannier tanks still within the shed appearing to be still in service.

After Oxley we headed over to Bescot shed (2F), which was an 8-track dead end shed and contained LMS or BR Standard built locomotives with more than sixty locomotives recorded. Bescot closed to steam on the 28th March 1966 being replaced by a modern much smaller diesel maintenance and fuelling depot.

Next, we drove through the centre of Birmingham to Aston shed (2J), only to find it had closed three weeks earlier, so we all stayed on the coach. It was unfortunate, as Aston was a large twelve track shed, the price of progress obviously. I suspect its allocation had been transferred to other local sheds, with Saltley possibly being the main shed to benefit. And Saltley shed (2E) was our next port of call, at the time it was a huge fairly modern steam depot with three connected roundhouses and virtually all full of steam locomotives. Like Bescot it comprised mainly former LMS and Standard built locomotives, however one surprise was the sight of a LNER B1: 61176 a York based engine at the time.

Tyseley shed was next and located on the south side of the city and still containing plenty of former GWR steam locomotives. The shed comprised a double roundhouse with obvious GWR origins and is now the base of the Tyseley Locomotive Works the former Birmingham Railway Museum. But back in 1965 it was home to over sixty locomotives mainly steam and thankfully twenty-seven former GWR types including eighteen still on the main shed with the others assigned to the scrap line and awaiting their final journeys. The shed still had GWR Halls, Granges plus Pannier and Prairies still operating from the depot. This was one of the main reasons we had booked on this tour and basically made it well worth the £1 booking fee.

Our final shed visit was Stourbridge Junction (2C) a former GWR single roundhouse with a 4-track dead end shed. The depot just oozed atmosphere and was a perfect end to the tour of Birmingham. With about fifty locomotives on the shed that day, contained twenty-four GWR types including a single Collett designed tank engine: 6129, which was basically designed for commuter work in places like Birmingham and London, a service now in the hands of modern DMU's thus making the tank engine redundant. I remember standing at the centre of turntable within the roundhouse, just taking in the atmosphere and enjoying what would soon be a frozen moment in time. Although, the UK has the benefit of many very professionally run preserved railways, the scene inside the roundhouse on that day in October 1965 is very difficult to accurately recreate as the dirt, grim, steam, oil, smell and light streaming in from the roof, creates a very special atmosphere.

After we departed the shed, I realised this would possibly be the last time I would visit a true GWR steam depot as the pace of progress would soon eradicate steam from the entire former GWR network, other than the remote outpost at Croes Newydd in North Wales. By 17.40 we were heading north on a hauled passenger service back to Manchester Piccadilly.

The next coach tour with the Buckley Wells was a North West event on the 8th May 1966 which visited Croes Newydd shed which by this time had been transferred to the LMR, so outside the control of the GWR management. Consequently, a small number of former GWR steam locomotives still survived in a land that time had forgotten. The following former GWR tank locomotives were still active on shed: 1628, 1638, 1660, 3709, 5605, 6697, 9610, 9630 and 9669. By the 8th June 1967 the shed had closed completely and finally brought the curtain down on GWR steam operation within the UK national rail network.

By the 12th February 1967, I had decided to do my first overnight coach tour covering depots in South Wales. This was a whole new world for me as we departed Manchester at 20.45 on Saturday evening travelling overnight to South Wales, first port of call being a number of stabling points in the valleys before visiting Landore depot (87E) and Swansea East Dock (87D) where we came across our first steam locomotives: 45004, 45058, 45138, 45430 and 76044 all on-route to G Cohens, Morriston for scrapping. After a quick visit to Margam Diesel depot (87B) we arrived at the now famous Dai Woodhams scrapyard at Barry Island.

The scrapyard was massive and basically comprised two main parts: the Upper and Lower yards plus an area close to an old railway building. The lower yard at the time comprised 111 steam locomotives including many examples that would be saved for future use on preserved railways that at the time these railways didn't even exist. The locomotives in the lower yard included two GWR Kings 6023 'King Edward II', 6024 'King Edward I' and former LMS Jubilee 45699 'Galatea' which I had previously seen in full working order during my first visit to Shrewsbury back in April 1964.

The upper yard comprised 41 steam locomotives including the second former Somerset and Dorset (S&D) 2-8-0 Class 7F's 53809, dating back to 1925 and became famous for their workings on the S&D. Thankfully the locomotives and the Somerset and Dorset Railway will not be easily forgotten because of the remarkable photographs and movie film taken by the truly great railway photographer Ivo Peters (BEM). I have a number of his films that detail the workings on the S&D, especially on Summer Saturdays when the line became a popular route for holiday makers heading to Bournemouth. Ivo took the time to ensure his work would be as near as perfect as possible and he obviously knew the best locations and the time of day to enable him to take the perfect photograph. He became very popular with many of the engine crews that worked the line, in addition to the sight of his Mk. VI Bentley car he used to ferry himself around the countryside.

Another ten steam locomotives were located close to the lower yard. This making a total of 162 locomotives, somewhat short of the two hundred plus locomotives that the yard contained at its peak. At the time of my visit, many of the locomotives were still largely intact and the task of saving them was in its early stages as individuals started to paint some of the locomotives to prevent further decay caused by the salty sea air. Also, painted instructions started to appear on the locomotives indicating that parts should not be removed and contact numbers regarding who was interesting in purchasing a particular locomotive.

BR Standard tank engines at Barry Island 80135 & 80079 on 12th Feb 1967. Both now thankfully preserved

It is now fully appreciated that if it wasn't for what happened at Barry Island, a huge proportion of the steam locomotives currently based on Britain's preserved railways, as well as many of those passed to work on the National Network simply wouldn't exist. So, todays railway enthusiast and preserved railways owe a considerable debt to Dai Woodhams for not making the task of scrapping the hundreds of steam locomotives he purchased from British Railways a more urgent task. Thankfully at the time he considered the job of scrapping thousands of coal and mineral wagons etc a more lucrative business. However, this still didn't stop Woodhams from cutting more than seventy locomotives that arrived at their scrapyard. Many suspect that these were scrapped as means of applying more pressure on individuals and preservation groups to speed up the process of purchasing their locomotives and removing them from his scrapyard. When you think about it, by reselling these locomotives it saved him the time and effort of scrapping them and I'm sure it made better financial sense but who cares as it gave the opportunity for individuals and groups to find the finances to purchase and transport their new assets away to their new homes.

After visits to Cardiff Canton and Cardiff Radyr depots which at the time still had examples of many diesel class's now just a distant memory i.e., Westerns, Hymeks and Teddy Bears Type 1 Diesel Hydraulics. Then we stopped off at Cashmores scrapyard in Newport, one of the scrapyards responsible for scrapping more than 900 steam locomotives during the 1960's and on this date, we could clearly see BR Standard built 76010 and 80033 awaiting to meet their fate while 76059 was virtually dismantled. In the centre of the yard was a huge mountain of scrap comprising huge chunks of steam engines including the smoke box off the front of a Southern Region Q1, which until then I'd never seen one of these strange looking Bulleid designed locomotives. On the return to Manchester, we stopped off at the recently opened Dowty Preservation Centre at Ashchurch and found Princess Royal 46201 'Princess Elizabeth' nowadays based at the West Shed at the Midland Railway Centre and former GWR Manor Class 7808 'Cookham Manor' plus 6697 both now based at the Didcot Preservation Centre.

After the South Wales coach tour, I only did two more coach tours on the 21st January 1968 Midland sheds and 3rd March 1968 a tour of the North West. The Midlands trip proved fairly depressing with just a few steam locomotives recorded during the whole trip: 61262 at Derby awaiting a visit to Arnott Young scrapyard in Rotherham, 75016 being used as a stationary boiler at Colwick shed, 47289 and 47383 at Westhouses shed following their work at the nearby William Thorpe Colliery and finally 61315 used as a stationary boiler at Staveley Barrow Hill shed.

The North West tour on Sunday 3rd March 1968 proved to be my last coach tour with the Buckley Well Railway Enthusiast and gave me a good opportunity to visit many of the remaining steam shed located within the North West. The tour only cost eighteen shillings and sixpence and almost certainly I would have met the coach at the Manchester pick up point at Victoria station. I still have most of the society magazines from that period, which is the main reason I can remember details like pick-up points and the cost of the individual tours. The magazine was a good source of information and from their regular shed visits gave you a good insight as to what was going on at the time i.e., shed closures and rare steam workings. The magazine for the first three months of 1968 reporting the sad news that Crewe South and Birkenhead sheds had closed to steam traction from the 5th November 1967, with the majority of the steam engines at Crewe slowly being towed away to various scrapyards whereas majority of those from Birkenhead were moved to Speke Junction shed. Consequently, this would greatly impact on the North West coach tour I had booked on. The rapid decline in the operation of steam the main reason why the North West tour would be my final trip with the society. I suspect the demise of steam also had a significant impact on other railway societies and possibly brought about a sudden end for many of these clubs and societies.

The North West coach first took us to Warrington Dallam shed (8B) which had closed during October 1967, so just two engines present 48053 and 45256, both awaiting removal for scrapping. Then on to Northwich shed (8E), which was just two days away from closing as an operational steam shed. Just fifteen Stanier 8F's present that day with most of them already stored and never to be steamed again.

After Northwich we arrived at Crewe for visits to the Diesel depot, Crewe South, Crewe North Stabling Point and the Works. Present on the diesel depot were a number of the new English Electric built D400 type diesels, which would soon take over the bulk of passenger services north of Crewe on the WCML to Scotland. The locomotives were built at the English Electric Vulcan Foundry at Newton-Le-Willows and were designed to operate at 100 mph and had 2,700 bhp available. So, when operating in tandem providing 5,400 bhp of power, when they were introduced to haul many of the express passenger services north of Crewe to Carlisle and Glasgow the BR planners had the means to accelerate the timings significantly. I remember seeing a pair of them blast through Carnforth station in the early 1970's whilst on a visit to the newly opened Steamtown Railway Museum at the former Carnforth shed and boy did they motor. Their combined power would have made the climb up to Shap summit look almost insignificant.

At Crewe South shed, the following were present: 60007 'Sir Nigel Gresley', 75029 and 92203 both the later locomotives had recently been purchased by the famous wild life and railway artist David Shepherd and were awaiting transport to their new homes. Whilst, 'Sir Nigel Gresley' had undertaken repairs at Crewe Works with its sibling 60026 'Miles Beever' denoting many parts to restore Gresley back to operate to main line standards. By now the depots at Crewe South, Croes Newydd, Chester and Birkenhead had all closed to steam operation. The tour would end up visiting two of the remaining steam sheds on Merseyside: Speke Junction (8C), Liverpool Edge Hill (8A) and finally Wigan Springs Branch (8F) which unfortunately had closed during December 1967 to steam but still contained a large number of withdrawn steam locomotives.

Speke Junction shed had eleven operational steam locomotives at the time of our visit and clearly remember the sad sight of Britannia 70024 'Vulcan' withdrawn along with about 45 other locomotives in the shed yard. Next, was Liverpool Edge Hill (8A), which I had never ever previously visited, God knows why I hadn't. That day seventeen engines were in steam on Edge Hill shed with Stanier Black 5: 45305 in absolutely immaculate condition, whilst Stanier 8F 48279 was actually in the process of being scrapped at the depot. The 8F must have been in very poor condition that prevented it from being hauled to a local scrapyard. The final shed of the day was Wigan Springs Branch (8F), which contained about 35 withdrawn engines, mainly steam but a significant number of old diesel shunters. Worthy of note were four BR Standard Class 4MT locomotives from a batch originally built at Horwich works from about 1953 onwards, so a maximum working life of just fifteen years. The engines were: 76077, 76079, 76080 and 76084, all being sent to Barry Island scrapyard, all but 76080 (cut up at Barry Island during 1972) have been saved with both 76079 and 76084 having been magnificently restored at and can usually be found at the North Yorkshire Moors Railway and the North Norfolk Railway respectively.

One of the other benefits provided by Railway Societies and Clubs was the running of special trains otherwise known as railtours. With the demise of steam and closure of many railway lines and branch lines, the availability of these special trains just took off. By the mid 1960's enthusiasts had the option to pick from a number of very interesting specials most weekends, usually employing some unusual motive power or covering lines soon to close. One means of advertising these specials was via a number of popular Railway Magazines, which were usually bought in those days from your local W H Smiths, especially those located on station forecourts. Even a relatively small society like the Buckley Wells Railway Enthusiasts got into the business of running railtours, usually in conjunction with another group or organisation and for example on the 28th April 1968 they ran the 'Lancashire Rail Tour' jointly with an organisation called 'G. C. Enterprises' and used Britannia 70013 'Oliver Cromwell' to haul the special via a circular route around the North West, starting and finishing at Stockport Edgeley station. The cost of the special was £2 and ten shillings and to be honest beyond my means, so I opted to visit Crewe on that day. Another railtour they were involved in happened on Sunday 20th November 1966 when in association with Williams Deacons Bank Club they used Southern Region Merchant Navy 35026 'Lamport and Holt Line' starting at Manchester Piccadilly and heading to Doncaster for a visit to the works then onto York for an organised visit to York shed. Again, the special was priced at £2 making it just too expensive for me. I was lucky to see Merchant Navy 35026 on Stockport Edgeley shed the day before the tour took place, enabling the staff at Edgeley shed to spruce up the engine for it special trip to Doncaster and York.

Running railtours towards the end of steam became a huge business and finally culminated in the final steam railtour taking place on Sunday 11th August 1968, when the infamous 'Fifteen Guinea Special' brought the curtain down on steam locomotive operation within the UK. The only exception to the ban imposed on steam operation being an agreement that had been signed that enabled The Flying Scotsman to continue to operate on the National Network. To take advantage of this historic event you had to stump up £15 and 15 shillings for the pleasure of riding behind a number of steam engines starting at Liverpool and heading up to Carlisle via Manchester Victoria station then returning to Liverpool. The railtour was assigned the famous head code of 'IT57' and covered a journey of 315 miles and even offered those lucky enough to be able to afford it, a dining option plus an extensive wine menu. Needless to say, as a sixteen your old and just about to start his first job the cost of fifteen Guinea's well outside my means.

When I started my first job at the Hawker Siddeley Aircraft Factory at Woodford, Cheshire I was paid a weekly wage was about £3 and 19 shillings, so 15 Guineas would have taken me four weeks to save sufficient funds and that was before I gave my Mum a huge chunk of my wage. Basically, the final steam special was for the privileged few, which certainly didn't include me. I had paid my respects to the end of steam the previous weekend along with thousands of other enthusiasts. Anyway, more about the end of steam later in the book.

Britannia's Locomotives

The sight of 70017 on the scrap line at Newton Heath on 20th February 1965 was not the end for this particular locomotive as it would soon be hauled to Crewe Works for a General Overhaul and was noted there on the 21st March 1965, then transferred to Carlisle Kingmoor to join an ever-increasing fleet of Brits at that northly outpost. The idea being that they would support the Type 4 diesels on services along the West Coast Main Line from Crewe to the north but the increasing arrival of Brush Type 4 diesels reduced their need for this role and by the end of December 1967, all the remaining Britannia's were withdrawn on mass, other than 70013 'Oliver Cromwell' which was retained for special railtour duties. This was a very sad end for a modern class of steam locomotive that were originally introduced from 1951. Consequently, some members only had a working life of 15 years or even less in the case of 70007 'Coeur -De-Lion', which was the first Brit to be withdrawn, following its visit to Crewe for a General Overhaul, but was obviously deemed beyond economic repair. So, by October 1965 it had met its fate and I actually saw the remains of it on the 10th October 1965 during a visit to Crewe when we first saw that Crewe North shed had been demolished other than the semi-roundhouse then onto the works for an official visit. Seeing the cab of 70007 plus other remains certainly brought it home that time was fast running out for steam operation within the UK. The sad sight of the remains of Crewe North shed and mangled chunks of 70007, confirmed my hobby was about to change dramatically and possibly made me more determined to see as many of those magnificent steam locomotives before it was too late.

The Britannia's were one of my favourite class of locomotives and I was always pleased to see them hard at work on an express passenger train or express parcel service. Originally the Brits were allocated to sheds across the country: Cardiff Canton, Strafford, London, Willesden, London and Polmadie, Glasgow, but the gradual introduction of Type 4 diesels, soon saw their duties being replaced by their modern alternatives. This then forced the first transfer of some of the Brits to alternative sheds e.g., March (East Anglia), Immingham, Holyhead, Trafford Park and Aston. But this was just a temporary arrangement, because by 1965, the entire fleet of Britannia's had been transferred to sheds in the North West of England: Crewe North/South, Stockport Edgeley and Carlisle Kingmoor.

During my visit to Crewe in October 1965, I recorded 17 different examples of the class including: 70010, 70013, 70016, 70027 and 70053 actually on the works, having either a general overhaul or repairs carried out, plus of course the first withdrawn example 70007. At this time Brits were still very active and on our arrival at Crewe we soon noted 70030 'William Wordsworth' arrive on a passenger service whilst 70038 'Robin Hood' for running light engine through the station. With the demise of Crewe North depot, Crewe South had become the new home for Brits at the southern end of their sphere of operations. On the depot that day was Britannia itself, 70000 in addition to 70019, 70020, 70023, 70028 plus 70029 and 70043 on the withdrawn or stored lines on the shed. Of these: 70043 was withdrawn and finally scrapped at Ward's scrapyard Beighton, Sheffield, whereas 70029 lived to see another day and possibly paid a visit to Crewe works before being transferred to Carlisle Kingmoor and was finally withdrawn during October 1967, just prior to mass withdrawals on the last day of December 1967.

My final memories of the class prior to that fateful date on the 31st December 1967 was a day earlier when I travelled up to visit two of the remaining steam sheds at the time at Lostock Hall and Carnforth and found 70021 'Morning Star' simmering away along with a number of other steam locomotives on Carnforth shed. I took a photograph of 'Morning Star', by then I fully understood its days were numbered. On the return to Manchester, I thankfully decided to head to Newton Heath shed and noted nineteen steam engines in steam, including Brit 70023 'Venus', which along with 'Morning Star' had just over twenty-four hours of life remaining.

70021 Morning Star at Carnforth shed 30th December 1967

Thankfully two Brits made into the preservation era with class leader 70000 'Britannia' and the final example to pass through Crewe Works for a General Overhaul 70013 'Oliver Cromwell' being the other.

The writing was already on the wall when the decision had been taken to build 55 members of the Britannia class and to be honest the decision to build 999 British Railways Standard locomotives during the 1950's was ill-fated, with some members of the huge 2-10-0 9F's barely having a 6-year working life. I'm not saying it was wrong to build these locomotives but maybe the BR Standard locomotives should have been given a better chance to pay back their original investment over a longer period of time, e.g., until 1975 at the earliest.

Britannia 70044 'Earl Haig' withdrawn at the rear of Stockport Edgeley shed 3rd December 1966

Family Holidays to the South Coast and Popular Music

I was extremely fortunate to have parents that not only had access to two caravans (one was Grandad's old caravan) in North Wales but also had the means to provide holidays on the south coast of England. The first holiday on the south coast I remember was during August 1965, when we spent about ten days at a caravan park north of Bournemouth. We drove down on the 9th August 1965 and by the following day I had persuaded my Dad to drop me off at Bournemouth station, where I stayed for most of the day and also found the time to visit the shed which was conveniently located directly opposite the west end of the main station platform. The main platform was extremely long to enabled two services to be handled at the same time. As a thirteen-year-old, the sight of all these Southern Region based locomotives was almost too much to handle and virtually all the express and local passenger services where still steam hauled. The bulk of the services from London Waterloo were handled by the magnificent Bulleid Pacifics either West Country/Battle of Britain or the Merchant Navy examples. Oliver Bulleid was the Chief Mechanical Engineer at the Southern Region between 1937 to 1948 and was responsible for the design of these Pacifics and was finally involved in the project to rebuild them from a streamlined locomotive to that of a more traditional design. The light weight Pacifics were known as West Country or Battle Britain Class and were either named after towns and cities located within the operational sphere of the Southern Region, whilst the Battle of Britain were named after parts of the RAF or associated with the Battle of Britain. Whereas the Merchant Navy locomotives were all named after famous shipping lines associated with the UK.

During the first two days of the holiday, I spent most of the time at Bournemouth station and took a number of photographs on my Kodak Brownie camera before I accidentally dropped the camera from a bench onto the floor of the main platform. The resulting crack in the body of the camera ruined many of the photographs I had taken earlier at Shrewsbury and those taken during the start of my Bournemouth holiday.

By the 15th August, my Dad decided to drive over to Weymouth to visit the town and its sandy beach. This was just too good an opportunity to ignore and offered a golden opportunity to visit the shed at Weymouth (70G). The shed was located close to the end of the station to the right and contained two Diesel Hydraulic Hymeks (Built at Beyer Peacocks factory in Gorton, Manchester) that I presume must have arrived on services from Bristol. However, on the shed was also a GWR Grange: 6870 'Bodicot Grange' which more than likely had also arrived from Bristol, unless it had arrived at Weymouth via one of the Inter Regional passenger services that passed through Oxford. My luck had obviously run out, as I had already seen this particular Grange during a number of earlier visits to Shrewsbury and Crewe South sheds and finally when it was withdrawn on Oxley shed Wolverhampton, awaiting its final journey for scrapping several month later in October 1965.

Weymouth shed still contained many Bulleid Pacifics including nine West Country/Battle of Britain light Pacific's and five larger Merchant Navy Pacifics and numerous BR Built Standard types. After the visit to Weymouth, I managed to squeeze in another three visits to Bournemouth before it was time to head home.

Bournemouth shed with 35023 and 34056 on the 11th August 1965

The next visit to the south coast involved a flying visit during the early part of September 1966 to our relatives who lived in Fareham. It helped when I discovered that Fareham had a regular train service to Eastleigh, home to a huge depot and railway works. By this time, I was fourteen and even more determined not to miss such an opportunity. So, on Friday the 2nd September and Saturday 3rd September 1966, I spent as much time at Eastleigh, obviously doing the niceties with my relatives, before legging it down the road to Fareham station. Eastleigh didn't fail to impress and was a hive of activity for steam plus the odd diesel including the sight of a Western Region diesel hydraulic Warship: D820 'Grenville', which then was a Plymouth Laira engine, so a long distance from its home depot. On both days I managed to get around the shed at Eastleigh and found it full of Southern based engines, including the unique former USA 0-6-0T tank engines. These engines had originally been built for use by the US Army but a number had found themselves transported to the UK, as a result of the Second World War and resulted in a small batch being purchased by the Southern Region, for work mainly at Southampton Docks, which were subsequently maintained at Eastleigh shed. On the 2nd September, 30067 was carrying out shunting duties in the yard alongside the station, whilst on shed was 30064. The following day found the previous days USA tanks had been joined by fellow class member 30073 and was photographed alongside the coaling plant on the shed.

30073 and an Ivatt Tank Eastleigh Shed – 3rd September 1966

During the two-day visits to Eastleigh, I managed to take twenty photographs and for once many of these photos were fairly reasonable considering the limitations of my camera. Thankfully the weather was excellent, which for a Kodak instamatic was essential if you wanted a half decent result. On the Saturday, I photographed West Country Class 34005 'Barnstaple' blasting through the centre road at Eastleigh station, with a Newcastle to Poole summer holiday Inter Regional express. This service would have used the former Great Central Railway (GCR) line via Nottingham Victoria and Rugby Central before reaching Banbury, where the locomotives would change and here the West Country would have taken charge for the run down to Poole. This was the last weekend that this service could have used the former GCR route as it closed to passenger traffic after that weekend. I was very fortunate to have the opportunity to visit places like Eastleigh and still have fond memories of the visit, plus thankfully some acceptable photographs.

My final holiday to the South Coast would take place approximately two months before the end of steam on the Southern Region when my parents booked a cottage in Swanage for two weeks.

Myself (on the left) and brother Peter outside the holiday cottage Swanage - May 1967.

We travelled down to Swanage on Saturday 13th May 1967 and returned home slightly early around the 24th May 1967. By this time, I was a Fifteen-year-old, who had no fear of travelling around the rail network, so Swanage with a rail connection to the main line at Wareham, was the perfect location. Wareham was on the main line from London Waterloo to Weymouth and at the time still had a good steam service. My first day of freedom came on Monday 15th May 1967, when myself and my brother caught the local service from Swanage to Wareham, then changed trains on to a London bound express that stopped at Bournemouth. I'm almost certain the first part of the journey from Swanage to Wareham was with a DMU but at Wareham the magnificent sight of West Country Class 34036 'Westward Ho' arrived with a full set of Southern Region coaches.

West Country 34036 'Westward Ho' ready to depart
Wareham station on the 15th May 1967

At Wareham we also found 34087 '145 Squadron' shunting the sidings, unfortunately bereft of its famous nameplates, but in otherwise immaculate condition. We were soon off to sunny Bournemouth riding behind a fabulous West Country Pacific, passing through Poole on route. Arrival at Bournemouth found the shed still very busy with steam but surprisingly the famously named Pullman service the 'Bournemouth Belle' arrived with a Brush Type 4 diesel, instead of the expected Merchant Navy steam engine. By this time the use of Crompton Type 3 diesels was a much more common sight on both passenger and freight services. However, I still managed to enjoy steam haulage for the return with BR Standard 4MT: 76069 providing a spirited run back to Wareham.

The following day I returned to Bournemouth, as per the previous days route and this time fell on Merchant Navy 35030 'Elder Dempster Lines' waiting for me at Wareham station, this was the first time I'd had the pleasure of a Merchant Navy for haulage. Once again, the Belle was diesel hauled, so suspect it had been diagrammed for Eastleigh based Brush Type 4. That day a couple of BR Standard tanks were operating passenger services towards Weymouth and I managed to have 80146, on my return to Wareham later in the afternoon. During the afternoon un-rebuilt West Country 34023 'Blackmore Vale' appeared and ran light engine onto the shed. The un-rebuilt versions were few and far between at this late stage and I was surprised one was still working, although the nameplates on the air-smooth body sides had been removed for safe keeping.

On the 17th May 1967, we drove over to visit our relatives at Fareham for a family get together. Needless to say, I was soon heading down to Fareham station and on route to Eastleigh. I suspect my two cousins must have thought I was fairly anti-social, with me disappearing soon after I had arrived at their home, but needs must! This time the shed had considerably less operational steam on hand with about nine locomotives in store or withdrawn including a departmental version of a USA tank engine DS233 the former 30061 plus fellow class members 30064 and 30071 located within the works. The final steam passenger workings of the day included 34001 'Exeter' work a passenger service through Eastleigh and finally 34098 'Templecombe' at Fareham on a passenger service.

Thursday 18th May 1967 was a repeat of the 15th and 16th May, this time West Country 34036 'Westward Ho' again took me from Wareham to Bournemouth. On this occasion West Country Class 34018 'Axminster' was carrying out the shunting duties at Wareham before the run into Bournemouth. The surprise that day was the appearance of BR Standard built 3MT: 77014, which at the time was supposed to be allocated to Sunderland shed, but from about the middle of 1966 had been working on the Southern Region, the whole class was either allocated to sheds in Scotland or the North East. It quickly became a celebrity locomotive and was used on a number of steam specials run on the Southern railway during the latter part of 1966 and until the end of steam on that region during July 1967. My return to Wareham was behind West Country 34104 'Bere Alston'.

34104 with a Bournemouth for Weymouth service - 18th May 1967
Prior to its departure from the far west end of platform 1.

On Friday 19th May 1967 my parents decided on a day trip to the beach at Weymouth. As usual I made my way to the shed at Weymouth only to find it a shadow of its former self. That day it contained just seven operational steam locomotives while six were stored ready for dispatch for scrapping. Noted at the station were 80146 and 73037 both still active on local passenger services.

My final day at Bournemouth station was on Tuesday 23rd May 1967, when I noted the following still working: 41224, 34093, 35023, 35028, 76005, 76067 and 80134 before calling it a day. That would be the last time I would see steam working on the Southern railway prior to its demise on the 9th July 1967. I took a very evocative photograph at the east end of Bournemouth station of modern Electro Diesel E6022 on platform 1, whilst in the background on the opposite platform, Merchant Navy 35028 'Clan Line' is ready to depart with the 12.35 departure to London Waterloo. Strangely, both locomotives made it into the preservation era.

E6022 and MN 35028 'Clan Line' at Bournemouth
23rd May 1967

Another memory of the holiday to Swanage was the day we visited Poole and found a local record shop. The front window of the shop had an impressive display using the recently released iconic Beatles album: Sgt. Pepper's Lonely Hearts Club Band as a centre piece of the display. My brother thankfully couldn't resist and promptly bought a copy. Surprisingly, Wikipedia reports that the album was released on the 26th May 1967 but I'm sure would have been on our way home by then, so we must have purchased a copy a few days in advance of its official release, unless of course Wikipedia has got it wrong! The most annoying consequence of the purchase was that we couldn't listen to the album during our holiday and had to wait to return home before playing it. No portable CD players in those days and indeed no CD's!

Whilst on the subject of music, myself and my brother were at the time developing a huge interest in music and had recently been bought a Dansette record player, which was at that time a very popular low-cost record player. They basically came in a limited number of colour schemes including Pink or light Blue with just two control knobs on the front providing either Volume or Tone control. They had two speeds for playing singles at 45 rpm or albums at 33 and third rpm and was about the coolest thing our parents had ever bought us! Mum and Dad surprised us on Christmas Day morning 1966 when they revealed they had bought a joint present for the two of us, a brand new Dansette record player, ours was a very fashionable Pink mixed with a shade of white. To say this was a surprise would be the understatement of the year and both of us just couldn't wait to visit our local record shop in Hyde, called Whites and Swales. I bought two singles: The Cream – I Feel Free (NSU on the B side) and a single by the Who – A legal Matter. During the visit my brother bought his first album i.e. The Byrds – Fifth Dimension. From then music just became a massive part of our lives and virtually every week we would be adding to our record collection. Soon we would be going to our first concerts, with many at the Manchester Free Trade Hall or one of the Universities or Colleges in the Manchester area.

The Cream – I Feel Free Single

To be honest by the end of steam during August 1968, my interests had switched from railways to music, with the John Peel BBC Saturday afternoon radio show becoming an essential part of the weekend's entertainment.

A few years later I replaced the Dansette with my first stereo music player, which had the luxury of two separate speakers and an additional knob for Bass control. I seem to recall it costing around £30 and was purchased from a music shop in Stockport. As the sum of £30 in those days was a significant sum, I had to pay for the player on the drip, which required my Mum to act as a guarantor. I suspect the bass and volume controls were usually set at maximum and probably drove my parents mad, as most nights I would be in my bedroom playing music, which must have sounded pretty weird to them.

How things have moved on, so much so that now at my age, I know exactly how my parents felt about the type of music we were playing at the time, as I generally have a dislike for music, that is today considered popular.

I still have my vinyl collections of albums and singles and to be honest, I just couldn't live without them, even though I very rarely play them. Music still plays a very important part of my life and there nothing better than going to a live gig, especially if it's in a small venue like a pub or small church hall etc. One such occasion was when I went to see an American Blues musician called Guy Davis, at a small music venue at Overton-on-Dee near Wrexham, and I was very fortunate to spend some time with him prior to the gig in a pub in the village.

Myself and the lovely Guy Davis in The White Horse Inn, Overton-on-Dee 25th November 2016

December 1967 to August 1968 - The Final run down of Steam

The 31st December 1967 saw the closure of the sheds in northern England at Carlisle Kingmoor, Tebay and Workington, plus the servicing facilities at Carlisle Upperby. With the earlier closure of Birkenhead and Crewe South shed to steam the area of operation for steam within the UK took a sudden turn for the worse. The British Railways senior management had accelerated the end of operational steam in the UK to finish during August 1968, with the remaining sheds being located entirely within the North West of England and centred on sheds in Merseyside, Manchester, Stockport plus those at Bolton, Buxton, Northwich, Wigan Springs Branch, Rose Grove, Lostock Hall and Carnforth.

The decision to bring forward the end of steam made me even more determined to play my part in recording the final run down of steam in the UK. With the knowledge that sheds at Carlisle, Tebay and Workington were scheduled to close on the last day of December 1967, I decided to visit the sheds at Lostock Hall, Carnforth and Newton Heath on Saturday 30th December 1967. This was my first visit to both Carnforth and Lostock Hall sheds, other than a very quick visit to Lostock Hall in the early 1960's when my Dad agreed to stop off at the shed whilst on route to Blackpool, but he would only allow me to walk along the end of the shed where the buffer stops were located and not venture down between the locomotives on the tracks within the shed. Unfortunately, I didn't keep a record of what I saw during this visit to Lostock Hall, which is why it had to be before 1964. Thankfully, former Preston Dock saddle tanks 47002 and 47008, were conveniently located at the end of the shed that I was stood at. Both engines were only allocated to Lostock Hall shed between September 1961 and September 1964.

Back to my trip on the 30th December 1967, the day started as usual with me completing my usual paper round, then catching a local service into Manchester Piccadilly then across to Victoria for a DMU up to Preston. On route, passing the shed at Bolton, which would stay open for the servicing of steam locomotives until the 1st July 1968, it had at least four engines in steam. From Preston, it was a local stopping service out to Lostock Hall station and a quick walk around to the shed. The shed had twelve engines in steam and eleven engines located on the sidings reserved for withdrawn engines. The bulk of the engines in steam were either Stanier Black 5's or 8F's plus a single BR Standard Class 5: 73132 and an Ivatt Mogul: 43019. After taking a series of Black and White photographs, including one of the Standard 5 as it moved of the shed, with my trusty Kodak Instamatic, I was on my way to Carnforth via a change at Preston station.

Carnforth was a medium size depot, with 6 through tracks, and dated back to the days of the London and North Western Railway and at the time had the shed code of 10A. Ten operational steam locomotives were on hand that day, plus a number out of use inside the shed and just short of thirty withdrawn engines occupying most of the available space outside the shed. These included BR Standard class 4's, Stanier Black 5's and 8F's plus a number of BR Standard 9F's. Also, on the shed were two preserved steam locomotives: 44027 (Part of the National Collection) and 46441 (Privately owned at the time by Chris Beet). These would eventually be joined by more steam locomotives that had been privately purchased as Carnforth became a storage area prior to the opening of many standard gauge preserved railways in the UK. As mentioned earlier, Britannia 70021 'Morning Star' was parked up in steam and would officially be withdrawn by the end of the following day. The Brit was still stored on Carnforth shed until April 1968, before being sent to Wards scrapyard, Inverkeithing, Scotland.

After Carnforth I headed back to Manchester via Preston then onto Newton Heath shed, where I found twenty engines in steam including Britannia 70023 'Venus'. By now the variety of types of steam engines still in service had been reduced to mainly Stanier Black 5's or 8F's with a small number of different British Railways built Standard types.

On reflection, I should have made the effort to visit the sheds at Carlisle and Workington on the 30th December, prior to their closure the following day, but that would have required another Saturday off my paper round plus more cash, so Carnforth and Lostock Hall it had to be.

Just two weeks earlier on the 16th December 1967, I had planned a similar first visit to Rose Grove shed (10F) which was located west of the Lancashire town of Burnley, on the line from Preston via Blackburn. Rose Grove eventually became one of the last three operational steam sheds, along with Lostock Hall (Preston) and Carnforth. On the journey north I noted a number of steam engines operating at Manchester Victoria station, including two BR Standard 5 types i.e., 73134 on a parcel service in Exchange station, whilst 73142 passed through Victoria station. Once again passing the shed at Bolton then onto Preston for a direct service to Rose Grove via Blackburn where I watched Ivatt Mogul (2-6-0): 43019 running light engine through the station. The Ivatt Moguls were affectionately known as 'Flying Pigs', and dated back to the late 1940's with 162 examples being built and were used across many parts of England, including: East Anglia, North East, Midlands, North West and Northern England. At this time very few remained in service and I suspect 43019 along with fellow class member 43106 were two of the last that survived until the middle of 1968. 43106 being the only member of the class that made it into preservation and is now based on the Severn Valley Railway and was still being used on the SVR as recent as 2020.

Rose Grove shed was towards the summit of the line that crossed the Pennines and provided engines for the freight services in the area, plus banking duties for the heavier freight trains over the Pennines. At the time of my visit the shed just comprised Stanier Black 5's and 8F's with twelve in operation either on the shed or working close by. As with many sheds at the time, its sidings were full of withdrawn engines, awaiting their final journey.

Ivatt Mogul 43106 now preserved on the Severn Valley Railway
12th April 1974

I suspect the return journey to Manchester was via Blackburn and direct to Bolton, where we saw the wonderful sight of Britannia 70045 'Lord Rowallan' working an express parcel service. Our visit to Carnforth two weeks later meant we had visited all three of the sheds that would stay open until August 1968.

Back home in Woodley it was good to see steam was still very much active and the daily task of shunting the yard at Woodley station was still in the hands of either a Stanier Black 5 or 8F from Heaton Mersey shed. As an example, the following were recorded shunting at Woodley: 45392 - 15th January 1968, 45253 - 17th January 1968 and 48546 on the 18th January 1968. The yard had a sizeable scrap merchants business located alongside the yard, which required the regular visit of a pickup freight to remove the scrap.

On the 21st January I visited the Midlands shed, on a Buckley Wells coach tour, which really did confirm that steam was now confined to the North West of England. A total of just four steam engines were noted during the whole day, none being in operational use. This trip basically made me even more determined not to book on any further tours that were outside the North West, as I wanted to spend the remaining part of 1968 enjoying the remaining months of steam. I just wish I had known more of what steam was working at the time, as in hindsight a number of services from North of the border still had portions from Preston to Liverpool which were still mainly steam hauled. If I had known, I suspect I would have made more of an effort to experience the final days of steam, especially those hauling passenger trains.

As mentioned earlier, I visited many of the remaining sheds, on the 3rd March 1968, on my last Buckley Wells coach tour. By this time, the curtain was fast coming down on active steam and virtually every weekend I was out and about in the North West recording as much as I could. After the coach tour, the two sheds in Stockport were visited virtually every week, including Sunday 17th March, when two railtours operated from Stockport to Carnforth, the first with the famous Gresley Pacific A3: 60103 'Flying Scotsman' and the second with Britannia 70013 'Oliver Cromwell'. Both railtours had been organised by the William Deacon Bank Club and were so popular that a second railtour had to be organised to satisfy demand for places. In addition, the recently preserved Jubilee 45596 'Bahamas' had arrived back at Edgeley shed following it overhaul at the Hunslet Engineering works in Yorkshire and was now painted in LMS Crimson Red. Bahamas along with the two engines used on the railtours to Carnforth were gathered together for an impromptu Open Day at the rear of Edgeley shed the day before the specials. So impromptu, that even I didn't manage to hear about it. The actual day of the specials I found time to visit both Edgeley and Heaton Mersey sheds with the latter shed being by far the busier.

On the 31st March 1968, I decided to take a final look at Trafford Park shed (9E) even with the knowledge it had closed to steam. The depot had five diesels along with ten steam locomotives all withdrawn and awaiting disposal.

Things were getting desperate, especially with the knowledge that my two local Stockport sheds would close during the weekend on the 4th and 5th May 1968. Consequently, on Saturday 6th April, Michael and myself first visited

Heaton Mersey shed to find twelve engines in steam and owing to favourable weather conditions, I managed to take some decent photographs, even with my basic camera. Visiting Heaton Mersey first was not recommended as it meant we had to walk up a huge hill to Edgeley shed later but that's how we planned it! The reason for selecting Edgeley second was that we knew a LCGB railtour was scheduled to pass the shed around midday, the railtour was named 'Lancastrian Railtour' and was hauled by Stanier Black 45305 throughout. I managed to take a photograph of the Black 5 as it passed the entrance to Edgeley shed, the resulting photograph also included Michael further down the steps also taking a photograph of the same special. That afternoon, 9B shed contained nine engines in steam plus seven inside the shed, out use. The rear of the shed found 44940 and 45038 awaiting disposal and were duly photographed along with many others who had taken the opportunity to photograph the special.

45305 passing Edgeley shed on 6th April 1968
With Michael taking his own photograph in the foreground

Thursday 11th April 1968, was the first day I recorded a diesel (Type 2 D7648) shunting the yard at Woodley, yet another nail in the coffin for steam. That weekend we drove down to the caravan in North Wales, only to find that steam had been completely eliminated from the North Wales coast and basically comprised Type 2, English Electric Type 4's and Brush type 4's on all trains. By Wednesday 17th April, the shunting duties at Woodley was once again in the hands a Stanier 8F: 48115 a Heaton Mersey engine that somehow managed to survive following the closure of 9F shed by being transferred to Rose Grove for the final few months of steam.

Saturday 20th April, we decided to make a return visit to the sheds at Lostock Hall and Carnforth. Once again travelling from Manchester Victoria to Preston then onto Lostock Hall passing Bolton shed on route. Preston still had a number of steam active that day, including 45212, which I suspect had worked a portion from Liverpool. Lostock Hall shed had six engines in steam including a BR Standard 9F: 92054. The sidings where withdrawn engines were gathered now contained many of the remaining Ivatt Moguls including: 43006, 43008 43019, 43027 and 43033, but no sign of the last remaining class member: 43106.

After a return to Preston, Carnforth was the next stop, where it was still very busy with steam and included an immaculate Stanier Black 5: 45342 which had earlier worked part of the RCTS 'Lancastrian Railtour No2' for the part of the special from Morecombe Promenade, paired with fellow Black 5: 45156 'Ayrshire Yeomanry' before handing over to 70013 'Oliver Cromwell' for the run back to Liverpool Exchange station. I managed to photograph the Brit at Preston station prior to it taking over the special. By this time Carnforth had become home for the remaining BR Standard 9F's with two out of use on the shed, whilst five others were all withdrawn in the sidings north of the shed building. In addition, Fairburn tank 42073 had been privately purchased and had made its way across from its last home shed at Normanton, Leeds. It would soon be joined by sibling 42085 with both Fairburn tanks destined for the proposed preserved railway at Lakeside and Haverthwaite, which was officially formed by mid-1970.

Stanier Black 5: 45342 on Carnforth shed
20th April 1968

After watching Cromwell simmer in bright sunshine whilst waiting for the arrival of the two Black 5's on the railtour into Preston, I was on my way back to Manchester Victoria station and saw both 44809 and 44910 stabled in the centre road at Manchester Victoria station, the location reserved for engines on station pilot duties i.e., for banking freights up the incline to Miles Platting. Later 44947 appeared in immaculate condition hauling a freight, this was at the time a Bolton engine, so the shed cleaners, or as was becoming increasingly common, a group of enthusiasts had given the Black 5 a thoroughly good cleaning. Yes, this was the level of dedication shown by enthusiasts at the time, they would form cleaning gangs and with the aid of ladders, buckets of water and plenty of cloths would set about the task of cleaning a steam engine from top to bottom. This action would be completely frowned upon under today's strict Health a Safety rules but just happened back then.

On the 23rd April I spent several hours at Woodley Junction photographing various steam workings. On Sunday 28th April, for some unknown reason decided to pay a visit to Crewe, with visits to the Works and depots at Crewe Diesel, South and the diesel stabling point at the former North shed. All I can imagine, is that it was a means to meet up with some friends, but the visit resulted in only one steam locomotive being at Crewe that day Gresley A4 Pacific 60007 'Sir Nigel Gresley' which by then was owned by the A4 Locomotive Society. By this time No 7 had received all three sets of driving wheels from fellow class mate 60026 'Miles Beever'. No 26 had been dragged down from Perth shed to enable the wheel set change to happen at Crewe.

BR Built 9F 92069 running light engine back towards Stockport 23rd April 1968.

The time was fast approaching for the official closure of the two steam sheds in Stockport. I decided the whole weekend would be taken up with numerous visits to Stockport Edgeley and Heaton Mersey sheds. First of all, on Saturday 4th May, I noted 45386 and 92160 working freights to Godley Junction whilst

45203 worked a freight on the line to Romiley, which must have originated in Manchester. Then it was on the bus to the centre of Stockport for a longish walk to Heaton Mersey shed which only had 48191 and 48723 in steam on the shed at the time of our arrival. However, three Stanier 8F's were busy on the freight line adjoining the shed, these were 48115, 48720 and 48356. The latter 8F carried a wreath on its smoke box and the inscription 'Last Day of Steam at 9F'. The shed was full of withdrawn engines which occupied many of the sidings around the shed.

Stanier 8F 48191 next to the coaling stage at Heaton Mersey shed
4th May 1968 – The last weekend of steam at Stockport

BR Standard 9F 92069 departing Edgeley shed
For the last time on the 4th May 1968

Then it was up to Edgeley shed, involving the climb up the hill to find only five engines in steam: 44781, 44871, 44888, 45046 and 92069. The 9F required new brake blocks fitting to enable it to return to Merseyside. Even with a new set of brakes the engine was withdrawn on arrival back at its home shed of Speke Junction. I suspect if it wasn't for the crew wanting to return home the 9F would have been withdrawn there and then at Edgeley shed. During our time at Edgeley two Stanier Black 5's were viewed working: 45269 light engine onto the shed, whilst 45312 worked a freight onto the sidings at Edgeley.

Then off back down the hill to Heaton Mersey shed to see if any additional engines had appeared and it was a resounding 'Yes' as the shed now contained eight engines in steam: 45282, 48115, 48278, 48319, 48356, 48687, 48723 and BR Standard 9F 92118. A number of staff were busy joining 48319, 48356 and 92118 together ready for their departure to new sheds. The shed was full of fellow enthusiasts, all paying their last respects to the shed and the engines it had played host to over the years. A very sad ending for a shed that had originally opened back in 1889 and was responsible for the supply of engines for the freights that worked through my home station at Woodley on route to Godley Junction and would soon be just a distant memory. I reluctantly decided to leave as the occasion was just too much for me and I headed across to Stockport centre to pick up the bus home. At Woodley I was lucky to see the three engines that had been marshalled together at Heaton Mersey shed pass through on route to their new sheds. 48319 was doing the hard work to haul the other two, with 48319 going to Bolton shed, whilst 48356 went to Newton Heath and 92118 finally on to Carnforth.

48278 on Heaton Mersey shed on the 4th May 1968

The following day Sunday 5th May after completing my massive paper round. I chose to pay a final visit to both sheds again, out of pure respect to the two sheds that had brought me hours of pleasure over the years. First port of call this time was Edgeley shed where the sight of four Stanier 8F's were ready to leave the shed for the last time, including 48115, 48191, 48278 and 48170 which had the task of being the last operational steam engine to leave the shed hauling its siblings to their new temporary homes. However, the scene ended with local engine fireman Tommy Baker walking in front of 48170 whilst playing a lament on his bagpipes as a fitting end of steam at 9B. 48170 then hauled its fellow class members over approximately a dozen detonators that had been placed on the track prior to their departure. Needless to say, the resulting explosions from the detonators was impressive and brought an end to Edgeley shed as an operational steam shed.

Next a walk down the hill to Heaton Mersey shed, to find four engines in steam: 45282, 48687, 48720 and 48723. However, a fault must have been found with 45282 resulting in it not being transferred away and was subsequently withdrawn from service at 9F, whilst the three 8F's all managed to leave, with 48687 being sent to Newton Heath, 48720 to Bolton and 48723 to Lostock Hall shed. Then it was time to leave. I have never ever returned to the site of Heaton Mersey shed.

Surprisingly, it wasn't the end of steam at Woodley Junction, as for a short period of time I would see a steam hauled freight on the line to Romiley usually with an engine from Newton Heath shed. On the 11th May: 48321 was on the freight working and finally 48620 was recorded on the 20th May, again a Newton Heath engine. That was the last time I ever saw a steam engine work any sort of service through Woodley. In time the line from Stockport to Woodley, would be closed and cut back to service an aggregates stone terminal at Bredbury plus the line across the Pennines via Woodhead would completely close, other than the short branch to Hadfield and Glossop.

The same weekend as the closure of the two sheds in Stockport, also saw the final two sheds on Merseyside: Speke Junction and Edge Hill sheds finally close to steam, resulting in just six remaining steam sheds in the North West i.e. Newton Heath, Patricroft, Bolton, Lostock Hall, Rose Grove and Carnforth.

I decided to make a return visit to Stockport Edgeley shed on the 24th May when I noticed the main shed building had been roped off, prior to the start of the shed building being demolished. They certainly didn't hang around in those days, even though the shed was still being used to stable a number of diesels, so it was still a signing on point for the engine crew.

All the remaining steam engines had been removed to the rear of the shed and included: 44836, 44855, 44868, 44940, 45027, 48182 and 48437. At the time of my visit Type 2 diesel D7550 was hauling Stanier 8F 48442 off the shed for its final journey to the Drapers scrapyard at Hull.

The closure of the sheds at Stockport left a huge hole in my life and surprisingly I never made an effort to revisit the three remaining sheds in the Manchester area i.e., Newton Heath, Patricroft and Bolton, all of which closed to steam on the 1st July 1968. I made a number of other trips including my Dad dropping me off at Derby for the day, whilst he visited a car auctions in Nottingham but to be honest my heart wasn't in it.

Then the fateful weekend of the 3rd and 4th August 1968 arrived when the three remaining steam sheds would officially close. I decided I had to visit all three sheds on the Saturday to pay my respects to the end of steam on British Railways. By now I had packed in my paper round and was scheduled to start work at the end of August, so no more begging the shop owner to allow me time off to do my hobby, RESULT! I had also finished school and unfortunately had lost touch with Michael, so decided to make my own way to the three remaining sheds. At Preston, I watched 45318 in steam in an adjacent yard, then 44806 passed Lostock Hall shed with a single brake van. Then onto the shed at Lostock Hall, which by the time of my arrival was like an open day, with so many enthusiasts visiting the shed. Thankfully, that day the authorities did little to stop them crawling all over the shed and I suspect it remained that way for the whole weekend. The shed had fourteen engines in steam, including the splendid Brit 70013 'Oliver Cromwell', which along with a number of other locomotives in steam that day were being prepared to work a series of six railtours the following day. Also, on shed was the last remaining BR Standard Class 5: 73069 which was scheduled to work with Cromwell on a Railway Correspondence and Travel Society (RCTS) special the next day. The shed contained twenty-two engines withdrawn in the sidings alongside the shed, plus another ten inside the shed including surprisingly Ivatt Mogul 43019.

BR Standard Class 5 – 73069 on Lostock Hall shed
Saturday 3rd August 1968

Britannia 70013 'Oliver Cromwell' on Lostock Hall shed
Saturday 3rd August 1968

After a return to Preston to see Black 5: 45231 on a freight, I then headed east to the shed at Rose Grove. Here eight engines were in steam, including named Stanier Black 5: 45156 'Ayrshire Yeomanry', all the other engines in steam were Stanier 8F's including 48278 with words 'The Last Copy Pit Banker' clearly visible chalked on it smoke box along with 48773 with its diagonal yellow stripe on its cab side, indicating it was prevented from operating south of Crewe, a little optimistic at the time. Again, the shed was littered with enthusiasts photographing and recording everything that was on shed.

Stanier 8F 48348 passing Rose Grove shed with a short freight
Saturday 3rd August 1968

Another return to Preston for a north bound service to Carnforth only to find hundreds of enthusiasts encamped on the shed. It would be interesting to know how much film was used over the whole weekend as it must have been a very profitable day for the likes of Kodak and Ilford etc. Of interest was the sight of two centre cab Claytons diesels D8523 and D8515 working a freight, the class would only have just over a couple more years of service when they too would be deemed fit for the scrap heap. In fact, D8523 only lasted until October 1968 before being withdrawn, a locomotive built during July 1963 and only existed for approximately five years and did little for the image of British Railways modernisation strategy. The shed had eight engines in steam, all Stanier Black 5's but slightly later the sight of BR Standard Class 4: 75019 arriving with a freight from the Quarry at Grassington was greeted by sound of hundreds of camera shutters snapping the last day this particular freight would be steam hauled. The shed was over flowing with withdrawn steam engines including the seven remaining BR Standard 9F's: 92077, 92088, 92091, 92118, 92160, 92167 and 92223. One of these 92167, had obviously had work done on it prior to it being withdrawn, resulting in the former 2-10-0 locomotive becoming a 2-8-0 with the rear driving wheels being disconnected from the other four driving axles. A number of the engines from Carnforth would be used on the final days steam specials including 45025 and 45390. In addition, the collection of preserved steam locomotives at Carnforth had grown to five including: 42073, 42085, 46441, 61306 and 75027, these would also be joined by 45025 and 45231. Finally came the time to return home passing the closed shed at Bolton, containing a small number of engines awaiting their disposal.

Stanier Black 5 45390 on Carnforth shed
Saturday 3rd August 1968

The following day I went to Stockport to see a few of the specials that were scheduled to tour the North West as a fitting end to steam. I had decided to go to Crewe with some friends, to tour the sheds and works for a final time, before saying good bye to my friends and bring to an end my days as a train spotter. I did however make a few more returns to Stockport Edgeley to see the sad sight of 44940, 45027 and 48182 awaiting their disposal.

After the end of steam, I did one further trip with my brother to the Farnborough International Air show that enabled my spotting interest to resurface. This involved boarding a special charter train at Stockport for travel to Farnborough. I obviously just couldn't resist writing down any locomotives we passed whilst on route to Farnborough. The biggest surprise was the sight of former GWR Pannier tank working in steam on the London Transport system near Old Oak Common: L95 (former GWR 5764), which is now preserved on the Severn Valley Railway and has worked for many years on the SVR. This engine, along with about a dozen more former GWR pannier tank engines, were employed on London Transport underground network on engineering trains until the final one was withdrawn during 1971. Six of these GWR Pannier tanks were sold to preserved railways including 5764.

Former GWR 5764 hard at work on the SVR
On the 11th September 1976

The Preservation Era

By the end of steam on the British Railways network a number of preserved railways were preparing to open their doors to the new era of preservation. However, officially the first standard gauge preserved railway in the UK was the Bluebell Railway in 1960, although it wasn't until 1962 when they began to operate between Sheffield Park and Horstead Keynes it has since developed into an eleven-mile railway with a northern terminus at East Grinstead. My first visit to the Bluebell came in 1979 during a visit to my Brother's home, at the time of our visit we enjoyed the sight and sound of former Southern Railways U Class 31618 and the tiny former South Eastern & Chatham Railways P class No 323 'Bluebell' at work. Further engines were stored on the shed at Sheffield Park, including the great sight of West Country Class Pacific 34023 'Blackmore Vale', which I had previously seen at Bournemouth during the final months of steam on the Southern Region.

The next major player in the world of railway preservation was the Keighley and Worth Valley Railway (KWVR) in Yorkshire, made famous by the film 'The Railway Children'. My first visit to the KWVR happened during the summer of 1970 by which time I had acquired my first 35mm camera. It was a Halina 35X Camera and was obtained by the exchange of Green Shield stamps. Back in the late 1960's and 1970's Green Shield stamps were a benefit provided by some shops and garages to encourage customers to shop at their particular outlet. Thankfully, my Dads garage was a Green Shield stamp outlet and as the interest in the stamps dropped off, he offered me the chance to use some of them to acquire my first decent camera. So early on in 1970, I visited the Green Shield stamp shop at Stockport St Petersgate where you could exchange your books of stamps for a variety of products which included a 35mm camera. The Halina 35X was made in China and was the first camera I owned that offered options such as: shutter speeds from 1/25 to 1/200 of a second and Aperture settings of 1:3.5 to 1:16. This took some getting used to as before it was just point and click. Now I had to take account of the shutter speed i.e., a fast shutter speed helped when photographed a fast-moving object like a train, which previously with my Kodak had been impossible to a achieve! By using a small aperture setting like F16, you gained a much better depth of field, meaning more objects are in focus.

After only previously using the likes of a Kodak Instamatic camera, it took a little while before I fully understand the art of producing a good photograph, not sure if I still do recall how to do this, as I now use a digital camera and tend to use the default setting to take my photographs. The only feature you tend to change is the zoom lens as the camera sorts any focus issues.

The first opportunity of using the Halina camera was during my first visit to the KWVR in the summer of 1970. That day, Ivatt Tank engine 41241 was busy providing a service between Oxenhope and Keighley, whilst at Haworth an increasing number of engines had arrived and the station yard now formed the railways main engineering and maintenance base. Haworth also played home to the first steam locomotive to be rescued from Barry Island scrapyard; Class 4F 43924, at the time numbered 3924. The railway had acquired a set of passenger coaches that enabled them to provide a service to the general public. The Ivatt tank, otherwise known as a 'Micky Mouse' had been purchased directly from British Railways and had previously been based at the shed at Skipton. After its purchase in March 1967, it simply made its own way down the line from Skipton to Keighley under its own steam, this was obviously before the ban on steam came into place after August 1968. As mentioned earlier the railway came to fame when it was used as the setting for the classic British film 'The Railway Children', which was released during December 1970, so the filming more than likely took place soon after the railway opened. The railway is now firmly established as part of the UK preserved rail network and has a very good track record of restoring former BR steam locomotives.

Class 4F 3924 (43924) at Howarth yard during 1970

Next preservation site I visited was the former steam shed at Carnforth, which by this time was known as Steamtown and housed a collection of former BR engines. I made my way to Carnforth in my first car a basic 850cc Mini, which my Dad had helped me purchase from a government car auction he went to at Ruddington, Nottinghamshire.

The site at Carnforth was extensive and enabled it to become an important base for restoring locomotives. It still contained a huge Coaling plant, operational Turntable and more importantly a shed to house its collection of steam engines. Today it is now the home of the 'West Coast Railway' and is the base for a huge collection of passenger coaches, diesel and steam locomotives. However back in 1972 at the time of my visit it was in an embryonic state and only contained seven former BR steam engines: 44767, 44871, 44932, 45231, 45407, 46441 and 61306 plus a former French Railway Pacific steam locomotive 231K22, which has subsequently returned to mainland Europe. I made a second visit to Carnforth on the 17th April 1977, using a Merrymaker charter train (Merrymaker trains were operated by BR and operated in many areas of the UK and provided day trips to places of interest) that started from New Mills and had pickup points at various stations to the east of Manchester including Marple, where I boarded the service. The train was hauled by an English Electric Class 40 and was advertised to offer passengers a chance to visit Steamtown or Ravenglass, where a famous 15-inch narrow gauge railway operated. The railway has the nickname of 'La'al Ratty' or more commonly known as 'Ratty'. I decided to get off at Carnforth, which meant I would be there for more than six hours. As a consequence, I had plenty of time to photograph their collection of steam locomotives including many famous engines, none more so than the 'Flying Scotsman', which was by then owned by Sir Bill McAlpine. Sir Bill had a passion for railways and thankfully the main person responsible for rescuing the locomotive back from America.

Alan Pegler originally bought the Scotsman from British Railways during the mid-1960s' and spent a considerable sum of money restoring the engine at Doncaster Works. By 1969 with the support of the Dept of Trade, he transported the engine to America with the aim of using the Scotsman on an extensive tour of the States for the purpose of promoting UK exports, which initially was very successful but a follow up visit in 1972, failed spectacularly and resulted in the engine being stored in an US Army Camp to avoid potential problems from creditors. Thankfully, Sir Bill began the expensive process to return the locomotive back to the UK, which he successfully did during 1973.

Many of the engines were displayed outside the shed building and also found former Stanier Black 5: 45407 hauling a number of preserved coaches within the grounds of the former shed, providing the opportunity for visitors to ride behind a steam engine. At the time you were allowed inside the shed building, which clearly reminded me of the days I would sneak around a BR steam shed but on this occasion with the blessing of the railway. Inside I photographed former L&YR Class 22 (former BR number 52322) dating back to 1895 and built at the L&YR works at Horwich. The locomotive is now based at the East Lancashire Railway at Bury. Also, inside the shed was former Rose Grove based Black 5: 44932.

Steamtown is now the operational base for West Coast Railways, which has turned the shed into a massive business and is home for a fine collection of steam and diesel locomotives, including two Jubilees: 45690 'Leander' and what many considered a lost cause; 45699 'Galatea', owing to its appalling condition but the skilled engineers who work at Carnforth, plus a considerable sum of money, enabled the locomotive to be returned to immaculate condition and is now a regular performer on specials on the UK rail network.

Next railway to visit was the former GWR shed at Tyseley, that at the time of my visit during April 1973, was called the Birmingham Railway Museum but is now known as the Tyseley Locomotive works and has an operating arm called Vintage Trains. The museum comprises of an operational turntable from the days it was a GWR shed plus buildings used to carry out very comprehensive repairs and rebuilds of steam locomotives. At the time of my visit, it was just starting along the difficult road to being developed into a highly respected steam locomotive engineering centre. Back in 1973, it housed about ten preserved steam locomotives including: two Castles 7027 'Thornbury Castle' and 7029 'Clun Castle', LMS Jubilee 45593 Kolhapur', two GWR Pannier tanks 7752 and 7760, GNR tank engine 1247 (Which is now part of the National Collection) and a couple of engines from the National Collection: SR Class T9 30120 and L&YR Class 5 (2P) 1008 (Former 50621) dating back to 1889.

After Tyseley, I drove across to the embryonic railway that is now known as the Severn Valley Railway (SVR). Earlier in 1970 the SVR had purchased 5.5 miles of track bed from BR starting from its northern base at Bridgnorth. The yard at Bridgnorth was littered with a number of steam locomotives, many in the early stages of being restored but also including some operational engines. The railway has now been extended all the way south to Kidderminster, with a rail connection to the national rail network at Kidderminster. It is now 16 miles in length and has developed beyond the most optimistic dreams into a huge business that comprises facilities that many other preserved railways can only dream about. For example, the railway built a massive new carriage shed with construction starting during 1999 and with support from the Heritage Lottery Fund delivered a 4-road covered shed building that is almost ¼ mile long and can house more than 60 carriages. In addition, two further roads either side of the actual shed building provide additional storage. This type of facility offers the railway incredible benefits to maintain and protect their huge fleet of heritage carriages and in recent years has become home to the Northern Belle rolling stock, a private luxury train operator that is famous for its Pullman style carriages and delivering the opportunity for customers to travel in style and comfort.

Like many other railways the SVR has built up a considerable engineering base for the repair and manufacture of new steam locomotives. The main base is at Bridgnorth but also includes the recently opened Diesel Maintenance shed at Kidderminster, which to be honest is possibly the best diesel maintenance facility in the whole of the UK preservation sector.

After my first visit to the SVR, I found time to visit its annual steam gala when the railway gathered together as many steam engines as possible and provided a specular gala for enthusiast. The railway now operates a number of steam galas a year when they regularly hire in engines from other railways and along with their own extensive fleet, provide a huge event that now typically operates for up to three days and now includes a night service, providing enthusiasts the means to recall the days when railways operated passenger services during the night.

The most local preserved railway for me at the time was at the Dinting Railway Centre, which became even more convenient when I moved from Hyde to Glossop. The centre quickly developed into popular railway attraction but was restricted by the size of its location. However, by 1974 it was home for a number of famous locomotives including: Jubilees 45596 'Bahamas', 45690 'Leander', Royal Scot 46115 'Scots Guardsman' and a couple of engines from the National Collection: Schools Class 30925 'Cheltenham' and GCR Class 04 63601 plus the benefit of visiting engines as the centre had a rail connection on the branch to Glossop. Visiting engines included: 'Flying Scotsman', 60007 'Sir Nigel Gresley', 45305 and 60532 'Blue Peter' to name a few. Unfortunately, Dinting Centre closed its doors during the early 1990's, for reasons I won't go into. However, it's good to see that land surrounding the centre is now being used for allotments and not houses as most people who lived in the area believed would happen.

5596 (45596) Bahamas at the Dinting Railway Centre
12th May 1974

The last preservation centre I visited during the 1970's was the Didcot Railway Centre, Oxfordshire which is located on the site of the former GWR shed at Didcot. The shed closed as an operational shed during 1965. The Great Western Society took over control of the shed during 1967 and by 1970 had negotiated a long-term lease with BR to enable them to use the shed as an operational base. I first visited the centre during August 1976 and found the centre well established and full of steam locomotives many that appeared in perfect condition and not like other railways at the time housing a number of derelict steam engines. The major problem with the centre is its location which restricts its field of operation and only allows for relatively short running lines; however, this does include both a standard gauge and broad-gauge sections of track.

GWR 6100 tank engine 6106 at the Didcot Railway Centre - 28th August 1976
The same class of engine I reported during
my visit to Stourbridge Shed in October 1965

The broad-gauge system (7 ft and ¼ inch wide) was the brain child of the famous 19th century engineer Isambard Kingdom Brunel who had grand plans not only to build a railway but connect this to his maritime business on the west side of England that would enable the public to travel directly from London to America by using his railway and transatlantic steamships. Unfortunately, his dream of a broad-gauge rail network was not in line with the rail network being built across the rest of the country, so in time his broad-gauge network was replaced by the standard gauge, which quickly became the norm across most of the world.

By my second visit to Didcot during June 1977, a total of fifteen former GWR engines were gathered together at the shed. During this visit I was surprised to find former Battle of Britain Class: 34051 'Winston Churchill' now housed inside the shed along with the other GWR fleet based there.

The UK now plays home to a vast number of standard gauge preserved railways and is a major player in the UK tourist business and as a result employs many thousands of people and is an integral part of the UK tourism business including international tourism.

The engineering facilities during the early days of railway preservation were somewhat basic and typically individuals had to work out in the open or inside old buildings that weren't ideal for restoring their locomotives but needs must and they got on with the job. This certainly isn't the case today when many of the larger preserved railways have extensive and very professional engineering workshops, including heavy engineering equipment to handle the repair and building of steam locomotives. In addition, a number of engineering companies now exist that offer highly skilled facilities to preserved railways and private owners of steam locomotives that are independent of any preserved railway.

Battle of Britain Class 34051 'Winston Churchill'
At the Didcot Railway Centre 28th August 1979

There are currently more than ten new standard gauge steam locomotives being built within the UK, following in the footsteps of those pioneer enthusiasts that built the Class A1 locomotive 'Tornado' back in the 1990's. Basically if you have the finance and engineering skills plus the determination anything is possible. Many engineering projects that at one time were considered just too difficult are now considered just routine but still very expensive. For example, the production of a cylinder block for a steam locomotive is now much more common, especially with the aid of Computer Aided Design systems to help in the casting as these huge chunks of metal, that in some cases can weigh as much as 5 tons. Some of the current or recent new build steam locomotives have used parts from other steam locomotives to form the core of the project. However, many of the new builds don't use any components from former steam locomotives, which obviously makes the project much more complex and considerably more expensive. Two examples of new build projects include the LNER Gresley P2, a huge 2-8-2 locomotive being built by the group who built Tornado. The other is the project to build a new BR Standard Clan Pacific: 72010 'Hengist' as none of the original ten locomotives built in the 1950's were saved. Alternatively, two projects using components from existing steam locomotives include 6880 Betton Grange, which has used the boiler from modified GWR Hall: 7927 'Willington Hall' as the centre piece of the project, whilst the project to build a GWR Saint Class has now completed, resulting in re-appearance of this class of locomotive that became extinct during the early 1950's. The Great Western Society based at Didcot bought former Barry Island resident GWR Hall: 4942 'Maindy Hall' for the sole purpose of using it to build a new GWR Saint class locomotive. This was successfully achieved during April 2019, when the project delivered the 78th Saint class locomotive and it has since moved under its own power at the Didcot Railway Centre. This must have been an amazing achievement for all those individuals who over the years used their skills and time to recreate this superbly engineered example of a locomotive not seen since 1953.

Life after school

After completing my GCE O Levels at the end of May 1968 my school took all 5th Form students to a swimming pool at Wythenshawe south Manchester. I suspect this was organised to prevent any pupils from engaging in any mischief on the last day at school. It was around this time, I packed in my paper round, resulting in me having lots of spare time on my hands before starting my first job at the Hawker Siddeley aircraft factory at Woodford, Cheshire. One sizeable task my Dad gave me was to sort out the rear garden of our new home in Woodley. Basically, when the house was first built, they simply bulldozed a load of clay on top of the top soil that previously existed before the estate was built. Dad suggested he would pay me if I removed all the clay and stored it to one side then dug out the soil hidden below and transport it to the top half of the garden. This would later be used on the borders around the top part of the garden, so Mum could plant some flowers in soil as opposed to solid clay. For several months I dug, dug and dug, using a wheel barrow to move the soil from the lower area I was digging to the centre of the upper part of the rear garden.

At the time I was starting to develop an interest in aircraft and our home was directly under the flight path into Manchester Airport or as it was called in those days 'Ringway'. To help with the new hobby I bought a portable VHF Transistor Radio that had the means of intercepting the communications between the aircraft crew and the control tower at the airport. In those days the aircraft crew would identify themselves by using the last three letters of the aircraft registration as their call sign. For example, British registered aircraft G-APET a B.E.A (British European Airways) Vanguard, would identify itself to a control tower by using: Papa Echo Tango, using three of the 26 code words used in the NATO phonetic alphabet. As no other British registered aircraft used the same last three letters, it uniquely identified the aircraft. That summer proved the start of a relatively short interest in aircraft spotting, which only lasted a short time. However, I still continued my interest in Military aircraft and would regularly attend the air show at Woodford, which in the mid 1960's had become a huge event and attended by tens of thousands of people. So much so that the roads around Woodford would become logged jammed as people dumped their cars and walked to the airfield at Woodford. I remember the first air shows I went to at Woodford with my parents must have been in the mid 1960's and on display that day at Woodford were representatives of all three members of the RAF V Bomber fleet: Vulcan, Victor and Valiant.

When I started working at Woodford during August 1968, a single Vulcan was still in the main top shed undergoing a major rebuild to extend the life of these magnificent aircraft for a further ten to fifteen years. The aircraft was the last example to receive this level of rebuild at Woodford and about a year later the aircraft was ready for its first test flight. The test pilot at the time must have decided to give all the staff at Woodford a spectacular display. When it took off for its first flight since the rebuild it virtually climbed vertical from the airfield at Woodford, with all four Rolls Royce Olympus engines on full power, an incredible sight and especially for those involved in the rebuilding programme.

Another very popular air show was at the RAF Vulcan Bomber base at Finningley near Doncaster. The show would comprise aircraft displayed on the ground allowing the public to see them at close quarters or in flying displays. Around 1970 the air show would always begin with the scramble of three Vulcans from the airfield. The sight of these magnificent huge Delta shaped aircraft taking off almost vertically into the sky above was just incredible and also deafening. I'm sure to enable them to take off so impressively they had their operating weight reduced to a minimum i.e., fuel etc. The scramble basically showed how these V Bombers would be deployed, if the county came under attack from a foreign power.

The air display included many current front-line RAF aircraft types plus some aircraft from foreign air force, like the United States American Airforce (USAF). However, the American aircraft were classified as all-weather aircraft and would occasionally not appear owing to poor visibility i.e. too cloudy! So, obviously if the allied forces were going to be attacked, it would obviously happen when it was cloudy, preventing the American Top Gun pilots from taking off!

As mentioned earlier the Farnborough air show became another regular event to visit, usually with my brother. I remember on one occasion, sneaking around a couple of aircraft hangers at Farnborough that were in theory off limits for the general public but didn't prevent me from being determined to see what was inside these hangers. In one we found a development of the Hawker Siddeley Kestral, code named the Hawker Siddeley P.1154 which was a supersonic vertical/short take-off and landing (V/STOL) fighter aircraft. We didn't manage to take any photographs as that would have caused major problems if we had been found inside the hanger. We would later in the day watch one of the RAF Harrier aircraft complete an amazing display, featuring the aircraft hovering over the airfield then moving backwards at slow speed. These aircraft just defied all conventions of a modern jet aircraft and I can still remember the news footage of them being used in the Falkland conflict, when they totally out gunned the Argentinian air force, so much so the Argentinians eventually refused to take on the RAF Harriers.

In the early 1970's I went on a number of summer holidays to my Grandad's caravan in Llanddulas usually with a close friend. The second, time, I went with a mate from work called Tony Kelso, who was definitely a massive enthusiast of aviation, so much so he once convinced me to do a coach trip to London and the surrounding area, including a few hours early in the morning at London Heathrow as the first Trans-Atlantic flights started to arrive. It was this trip that convinced me that this new hobby wasn't for me. However, during our holiday to North Wales, we visited a number of RAF bases in the area, including Valley and Llanbedr. At Valley we watched a Vulcan carryout a touch and go landing but didn't actually touch the runway. This was closely followed by a USAF F111 Aardvark a fighter bomber. Then Tony suggested we try and see the part of the airfield where RAF Lightnings were loaded with live missiles for use on the firing range in Pembrokeshire. This involved walking along the beach then crawling up an embankment so we could see the aircraft have their weapons loaded. I'm surprised we didn't get caught and accused of being Russian spies!

After safely returning to my car, we drove off the island of Anglesey and headed down the coast through Harlech to the RAF camp at Llanbedr. Visiting this place was like going back in time, with a range of the early jet aircraft being used that day, including Canberra, Gloucester Meteor, Hawker Hunter and the odd propeller aircraft as shown below:

Avro Anson at Llanbedr Airfield

My first year at Woodford, involved working within the Engineering training school, which comprised three sections: Fitting Room, Machine Shop and class room for theory. Students would be given tasks to make their own tools and finally if you completed making all your assigned tools, you were allowed to make a tool box to accommodate the tools you had made. I did manage to make my own tool box but was the last student to make it from steel plate as opposed to lightweight aluminium, the weight difference being very noticeable. The machine shop offered the chance to use lathes, vertical millers and horizontal metal grinders to make various tools.

After a year in the training school, completing that part of my apprenticeship I along with most of the other apprentices were transferred to work on the shop floor. Unfortunately, not all the apprentices were lucky to continue on to the shop floor and were told they didn't make the grade to continue.

At the time Woodford was making HS 748 a medium size Turboprop passenger aircraft plus the Mk1 version of the maritime patrol aircraft Nimrod, which would replace the ageing Avro Shackleton, which to a lesser mortal had the look of a Lancaster bomber or similar. I was placed with a couple of aircraft engineers who were working on the Nimrod production line and their main task was installing the heating system within the bomb bay, which supplied heat from the jet engines to prevent the bomb bay from freezing up. The heating system ran the entire length of the bomb bay. I must admit the experience of working on the shop floor was interesting to say the least and certainly opened my eyes to what life was like at the time.

The Nimrod production line at Woodford during the 1970's

Around this time Woodford employed a system called 'Piecework', which involved the shop floor workers negotiating the time to complete a particular job with staff called Rate Fixers. The Rate Fixers, were managements attempt to try and control costs of building an aircraft but in many cases, it appeared to inflate the cost when the Rate Fixers didn't fully understand the scale or complexity of a particular job. The main task for the guys on the shop floor was to get as many hours as possible to complete a job, whereas the Rate Fixer would be trying his best minimise the cost and time of a job. The two guys I worked with were very good at convincing the Rate Fixer to give them more than sufficient time. One particular job that I remember well took place during overtime and required a drainage nozzle riveting to the nose of a Nimrod aircraft. To be honest the job was made much more difficult as there wasn't sufficient room inside the nose of the aircraft to easily position and fix the drainage nozzle at the correct place as shown on the engineering drawings used to complete the task. This required lots of fiddling and cursing to get the item correctly aligned as your fingers just got in the way. However, this particular evening the guys decided to leave me to carry on with the task whilst they went for a brew. They just couldn't believe their eyes when they returned to not only find I had managed to perfectly rivet the item to the nose of the aircraft but also connected the pipework to enable the drainage system to work. As they had already negotiated many more hours to complete the task as agreed with the Rate Fixer, they couldn't be seen to complete the job so quickly. Consequently, they forced me to disconnect the pipe work and remove three of the rivets that held the item in place and told me to stop rushing the job! Needless to say, I was not too impressed and told them to get on with the job on their own.

When an apprentice started working on the shop floor, the engineers they were assigned to work with would often try to make fools of the apprentice by sending them on stupid tasks. This usually involved the apprentice being sent to the central stores located within the factory where you collected parts or tools required to build the aircraft. However, there were a number of these so-called engineers that used this as an opportunity to humiliate their apprentice. For example:

- Go to stores for a long weight (wait)
- Go to stores for a long stand. (standing about)
- Go to stores for a tin of Yellow and Black striped paint.
- Pass me the Left Hand Screw Driver

Unfortunately, there were one or two apprentices that just didn't seem to understand what was happening, especially one individual with a Polish name from my year's intake. He unfortunately appeared to spend most of his time waiting outside the Stores. A number of us would try and help him by telling him what was going on but he was just too timid to do anything about it.

The two guys I worked for tried their best to get me to do a number of stupid tasks, until one day me and a mate who also was working on the same aircraft inside the bomb bay, actually wrestled the one that was the most annoying to the ground and basically told him to stop treating us like idiots. His mate just stood by whilst we made his colleague agree to treat us with some respect, surprisingly he did agree and that was the last time he ever tried it on with us. Not the best thing to do as if a foreman had caught us, we would have more than likely been sacked on the spot but occasionally you have to draw a line under a problem and thankfully it worked for both of us. This problem is now known as 'Bullying', which in those days was just endemic in places like Woodford.

Another incident I remember too well was when I was assigned to work with a team who were responsible for working on Victor Bombers after they arrived from the former Handley Page factory at Radlett. Handley Page had recently gone out of business and the job of converting the Victors to flight refuelling aircraft was awarded to Hawker Siddeley. However, the conversion work had to be delayed owing to the huge amount of work being undertaken at Woodford at the time. So, the Victors had to be made safe for a period of storage and involved the removal of many electrical items. One of these items was located within the wing of the Victor and required a person to climb in to the inside of the wing via an inspection hatch from inside the undercarriage bay. In those days I was very tall but also extremely slim, whereas the majority of the older men in the team were not so slim. Consequently, I was asked to carry out the task of removing a number of electrical items from inside the wing. I had completed a number of these and just managed to get into a small enclosed area inside the wing where the items were bolted down. Anyone who suffers from claustrophobia would fully understand my fear of doing this job but you just got on with it.

However, on one sunny hot day I was again asked to do the job and this time managed to get stuck in the wing as the heat had made me expand and I just couldn't turn around to exit the confined space. Luckily one of the guys had stayed at the opening that I had climbed in via and heard me starting to panic. He suggested that I reverse out of the wing without turning around i.e., feet first. Eventually I started to move and the relief when my feet popped out of the inspection hatch was immense and got better when two guys started to pull me out of the hatch. That was the end of my visits to the inside of a Victor Bomber wing and to be honest wasn't a job an apprentice should have been asked to complete.

The apprenticeship involved a day release and one evening at Macclesfield college where apprentices were assigned to a number of engineering courses. I was fortunate to be placed on a course that gave me the chance of starting an Ordinary National Certificate (ONC) Mechanical Engineering course. Thankfully, I did achieve the grade necessary and started the ONC course a year later. This was a two-year course and covered subjects like Thermal Dynamics, Mechanical Engineering, Electrical Engineering etc and if you achieved an average result of about 65% across all subject you would qualify for a place at Salford University on an BSc Aeronautical Degree course. Salford University at the time had significant ties with Hawker Siddeley and the British Aircraft Corporation, owing to the Engineering Faculty having an Aeronautical school, for potential high flyers! Sorry just couldn't resist the pun!

After a lot of hard work and hours of revision, I actually achieved an average mark of about 80% with a 92% success in Mechanical Engineering, which even surprised me! The education department at Woodford offered me the chance to go to Salford University on a 4 year sandwich course comprising 3 years involving 6 months at University and 6 months at Woodford, whilst employed in various departments within the factory. Although one of these work experience assignments, I actually worked in the wages department, which involved making up shop floor workers' pay packets on a Friday. When I had my regular meeting with my course tutor at Salford and told him I was in the wages dept, he was somewhat surprised and confirmed he would speak to the appropriate staff at Woodford. He was obviously a man of his word as a few weeks later I was transferred to the Carbon Fibre test unit. Then the final year you completed a full academic year whilst undertaking your assigned project. My course tutor offered me a number of projects but the one that appealed to me the most involved building a test rig to carryout thermal stress strain analysis of a square aluminium plate with the thermal stress being created by heating one side of the plate, whilst cooling the other therefore inducing a stress in the plate. This would simulate the surface of an aircraft wing whilst flying at high-speed causing friction as it passed through the atmosphere. A series of thermal strain gauges would transfer any changes in the plate to a piece of equipment that recorded the thermal changes within the aluminium plate. The data from this was then sent for analysis and input into a programme run on a mainframe computer system based at Manchester University, resulting in a paper readout of the whole operation. My project course leader had written the programme that I used at Manchester and was impressed with my work and the results, especially when I had produced my final year thesis which resulted in my degree being awarded.

One benefit of making my rig to carry out these tests was that I was required to photograph the equipment for inclusion in my thesis. The lab technicians allowed me to use the dark room facilities within the Engineering Faculty. I took full advantage of these facilities and made prints from a number of my early 35mm negatives I had taken at the Keighley and Worth Valley Railway. Its very pleasing to see your negatives develop into a photograph right in front of your own eyes.

I actually made the end structures that would either heat or cool the plate, this would normally have been done by the technicians in the Faculty Engineering labs but as I had been trained in the use of vertical Milling machines, I did the job myself, with a technician overseeing the work whilst I operated the machine. To be honest the lab technicians were really helpful and did assist in the setting up of the equipment, I suspect more out of curiosity they found time to oversee the experiment when I eventually started to operate the rig.

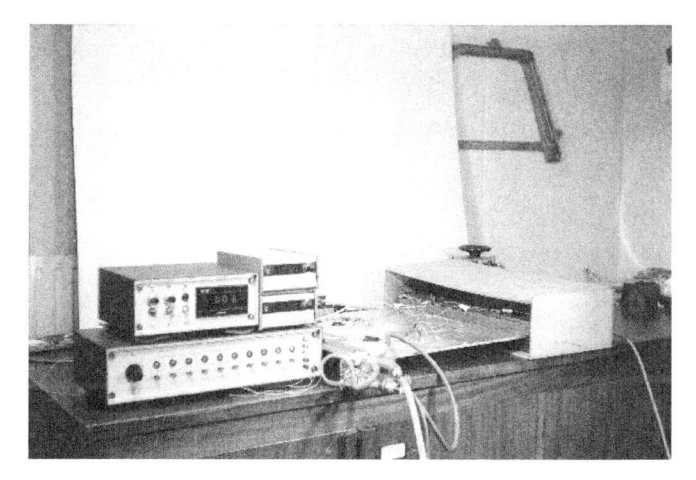

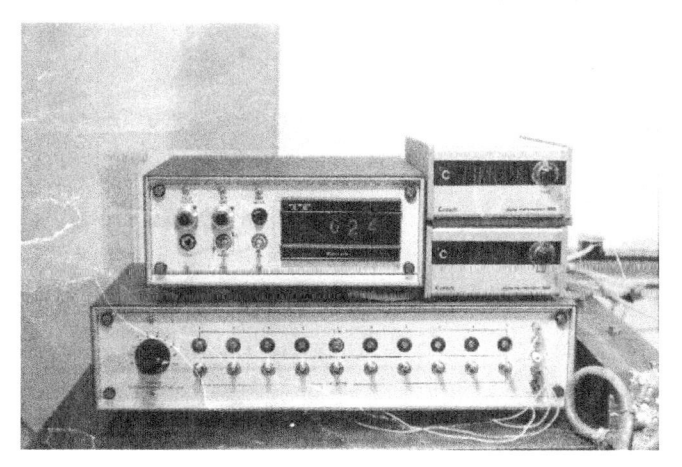

Three photographs of my final year project test rig.

After completing my degree, I returned to Woodford and was offered the chance to work within the recently formed Computing Services Dept, even though I had done very little computing at Salford. These were the very early days of computing being used as a tool within industry and I was extremely lucky to be given the opportunity.

I was even more fortunate to be given the chance to work on a project that involved computer graphics, using the scientific programme language Fortran and a graphics package called GINO-F (Graphical Input/Output – Fortran). The graphics package was a toolkit of subroutines and functions that allowed you to draw 2D and 3D graphics. The department had a single Tektronix 4010 Graphics Terminal, which was linked to their ICL 1900 Mainframe at their Chadderton factory near Oldham. I had virtually sole use of the Graphics Terminal but found it extremely difficult to get the 1900 to perform any sort of task over a slow communications links. An example of how slow the mainframe performed, is that I would start to compile my source code in to an executable programme as I went for lunch then would return from lunch and play a few games of Bridge before checking if the compilation had completed. The answer would be 'NO' and I would have to wait longer for this simple task of a compilation to complete. This would then allow me to run the executable program that I had just created to see if my programming had worked.

Myself and another programmer were asked to develop one of the first systems using computer graphics to deliver an engineering project, my colleague did the number crunching calculations, whilst I did all the graphics works. Eventually we were asked to demonstrate the project to a number of staff from other engineering divisions within Hawker Siddeley, I had warned my Head of Department and line manager that the ICL 1900 was just not good enough to deliver the task, which on the day of the demonstration proved to be the case. The demo simply stopped half way through the exercise, even though the Head of Department had arranged for a dedicated link to the mainframe in an attempt to stop it causing problems. The failure of the demonstration resulted in the project being transferred from the ICL Mainframe to a Dec PDP 11 that was located in a laboratory near the shop floor. The transfer took both of us a considerable time to complete and actually involved a number of weekends, so plenty of overtime, which helped as I had recently got married and was settling into our new home. The transfer worked perfectly and proved to the senior management how useful computer graphics could be to deliver a project of some complexity on the right type of equipment.

A Tektronix T4010 Graphics Terminal

I spent two years at Woodford working in the Computing Services Department, before I realised, I needed to move on and resulted in me being successful in the appointment to a post at The University of Manchester Institute of Science (UMIST) for a Government Research Project called the Interactive Computing Facility (ICF) the project was funded by the Science and Engineering Funding Council and had two centres at Manchester and Edinburgh using Dec System 10 mainframes. Initially I was appointed as a User Support Programmer but within a year had become a Senior User Support Programmer then eventually the User Support and Operations Manager responsible for not only staff based at UMIST but staff located at many other Universities across the country. The task was to develop and promote computer graphics as a tool to the academic community. The Dec

System 10 would be replaced by a network of Prime Super Mini computers which I was also responsible for plus the staff operating them. This was a very exciting time in my life and required lots of travel across the country to support and manage these facilities.

The UMIST Dec System 10 with the Operator console in the centre

Part of the Prime Super Mini Computer that replaced the Dec 10 system

The photograph shows part of the system i.e., Disk and Magnetic Tape Drives

Never one to sit still, I applied for a job at Shell UK main computing centre at Wythenshawe, Manchester, After, various tests I was appointed to a post in their UNIVAC support group, which I soon found to be a poor decision on my part. The task and challenges involved in the group I was working, were just too uninspiring and soon I was looking for a way to leave. However, whilst at Shell, I had an opportunity see their main UK computer centre which was very impressive and housed their IBM and UNIVAC main frames in a number of very expensive computer rooms, whilst in a corner was a very impressive Cray super computer. A Cray was at the time one of the most powerful systems designed to handle huge amounts of data and used in the analysis of weather or geological data and its appearance was equally as impressive.

Shell used a Cray for their geological exploration analysis and they looked nothing like any mainframe computer I had ever seen before.

Whilst all this was going on, I had got married at the end of my third year at Salford University, bought our first home and by 1977 moved to our second home and three years later our first daughter Lisa was born, followed two years later by Stephanie, both becoming a wonderful part of my life.

My daughters aged 4 and 2.

Renewed interest in railways

Whilst working at UMIST I started to travel extensively with my job and it was those journeys that retriggered my interest in railways, which I thought I had left behind at the end of steam in 1968. I think the real reason for the resurgence was the knowledge that the magnificent Deltics were fast coming to the end of their reign on the East Coast Main Line. I made a number of trips to York to photograph them whilst working the semi fast service from Kings Cross to York. In addition, many of my business trips to London eventually involved a diversion across to Doncaster for a journey to Kings Cross behind a member of the class. The return usually involved catching the 16.05 from Kings Cross north to Doncaster and provided the chance to listen to the awesome sound and power of the two Napier engines blasting years of soot off the roof of the Copenhagen tunnels as you exited Kings Cross station. By the 2nd January 1982 a railtour was run from Kings Cross to Edinburgh and return as a farewell to the class. I made the effort to say farewell to the Deltics by travelling to York that day along with hundreds of other enthusiasts. Unfortunately, the day was a typical British winters day and day light was virtually non-existent, so taking a well-focused photograph was impossible even with a half decent SLR camera. The return of the railtour to Kings Cross station actually made it on to that evenings BBC National News and clearly showed how popular these modern diesels had become with one well known enthusiast filmed kneeling down next to the Deltic and kissing the nameplate of the locomotive. I shan't mention any names just in case his family is unaware of what happened, your secret is safe mate!

By 1980 I had joined a new Railway Society based in the North West called the Lancashire Locomotive Society (LLS), which ran coach tours all over the country plus a number of railtours. My first coach tour with the LLS was over the weekend of the 14th and 15th February 1981 covering depots and stabling points on the east side of the England. After being picked up at Manchester Victoria station we headed east towards our first stop at Lincoln, then onto Boston and eventually visiting numerous depots and stabling points until we reached the British Rail complex at Stratford which included a depot and workshop. This was the first time I had ever visited this part of the UK and I was especially impressed with the visit to Stratford.

The next event I booked on was a visit to the former GWR works at Swindon, which by this time had just become a dumping ground for redundant diesel locomotives, with numbers of Class 25's, Class 40's, Peaks etc now arriving for storage or scrapping. The trip was completed by using trains to reach Swindon. I continued to take advantage of the LLS trips until I was eventually invited to become a committee member, which I duly accepted and was given the responsibility of managing the sales side of the society i.e., food and drink plus book sales on the coach tours. About this time, we began to get involved in the running of railtours and formed a partnership with a group called T&N (Terry Waterhouse and Neil McCann) to run a number of very memorable railtours.

The first railtour I was involved with was the running of the 'Devonian' from Preston to Paignton on Bank Holiday Monday 28th May 1984. The day before the running of the railtour, myself and society chairman; John Birch, visited Longsight depot to ensure that two Class Forties would be available. The depot foreman, reported he was doing his best to have D200, the celebrity class member manoeuvred to Longsight so it would be available to work the railtour. We told not to bother as we already knew this particular locomotive would work huge numbers of railtours in the coming years. So, we requested 40057 along with 40135 as the best pair that were on hand at Longsight depot that day.

The event had been advertised to run with a pair of Class 40's to the west country then top and tail Class 31's along the Heathfield branch, whilst the Class 40's were serviced at Exeter. I managed the sales stand in the rear brake coach where various food and drink options were offered plus the LLS sales stand whilst Neil sold beer which unsurprisingly proved to be very popular as the day became fairly hot and sticky.

As predicted, 40057 and 40135 arrived at Preston to work the railtour south, with both working well on the southern leg of the special but on the return began to cause serious problems, so much so that they were removed at

Bristol Temple Meads in favour of Class 47: 47199, which didn't amuse the bulk of the customers on board the train. Attempts were made to have the 47 replaced, which proved successful when we reached Crewe to find 40177 waiting to replace the unpopular Class 47. The Class Forty completed the final part of the railtour to its final destination at Preston and I had the pleasure of a cab ride before arriving back at Preston.

The tour proved to be very popular and resulted in a series of similar events being run. Unfortunately, it was the running of these railtours that eventually caused the committee to split, especially after one committee meeting prior to the running of the 'St Andrew II' railtour. Six weeks prior to the date of the proposed railtour the bookings were not looking good and it was suggested that we cancel the running of the railtour. After a long discussion myself and the chairman John Birch both wanted to continue with the tour whereas the other three committee members wanted to cancel and that was the final decision. However, as John was handling all the bookings and I was assisting him with the running of the event we made the decision to just continue with the railtour. Two weeks before the event John informed the other committee members that we were pressing on and invited them to joins us in running the railtour on the 24th April 1985.

Surprisingly they all did and the railtour went ahead, starting at Bolton and travelled north to Edinburgh, then a series of mini tours around the central part of Scotland. The tour proved a considerable success and actually broke even in the end. Unfortunately, the running of the railtour had created cracks within the committee, resulting in both myself and John resigning, which was a sad result as the LLS was at the time a very well-run society and highly regard by many of my friends who were members of the group. But that's life and you just have to move on.

Part of the committee during an Open Day at Crewe Works on 2nd June 1984.
Martin Birchall, Myself, Dave Shirley and Brian Hurst
Including on display the Head Board used on the Devonian Railtour

The Devonian railtour whilst at Bristol Temple Meads station.
This photograph was sent to me by a fellow enthusiast who took the photograph but unfortunately, I can't recall his name.

The actions of John and myself, prevented the cancellation of the final railtour the society would run and ensured that all seven railtours organised by the society actually all ran as advertised. The first railtour the LLS ran was back in April 1980 with the 'St Andrew II' being the last.

With no involvement in the LLS, I found I had more time on my hands and regularly went to railway line at Chinley, Derbyshire on a summer Saturday to photograph the Manchester to Skegness and Manchester to Yarmouth summer holiday services plus the many freight services that ran at that time. Plus, more time to enjoy with my lovely daughters, who would come with me on many of my adventures.

The family holidays were usually taken in Devon at places like, Torbay, Dawlish and Teignmouth as the railway conveniently ran directly alongside the Devon coast and enabled my daughters to enjoy the sea and myself the opportunity to photograph anything that passed by on route from Exeter to Newton Abbott.

50046 passing Dawlish during July 1984

By September 1985, I decided to take a weeklong visit to Scotland. This was the first time I had spent so long away from home and was made possible by using a Scottish Rover ticket, which enabled a weeks unlimited travel on all services in Scotland. My earlier interest to travel behind the Deltics, transformed me from basically being a Train Spotter into what is now known as 'A Basher' i.e., an individual that is interested in travelling behind locomotives and not simply writing numbers down. This development within the hobby of railway enthusiasm become extremely popular during the 1970's and 1980's and resulted in a number of companies appearing that offered specialised railtours for the enthusiast market, using locomotives that normally wouldn't work passenger services, typically freight locomotives. These companies now offer many services to the general public including the chance to ride behind famous steam locomotives.

The trip to Scotland, basically super charged my interest in haulage which would eventually see my travelling all over Europe and North America in pursuit of my hobby. However, back to the Scottish trip, I planned to cover as many interesting passenger services in Scotland including many lines that I had never previously travelled on. During the weeklong trip I based myself at a Bed and Breakfast close to Haymarket in Edinburgh. With one overnight visit to Inverness half way through the week, which would allow me to sample the recently introduced English Electric built Class 37's diesels on the lines radiated from Inverness to Kyle of Lochalsh, Wick & Thurso and Aberdeen.

Back at Haymarket, the B&B was managed by a former army person, who knew exactly how to cook an impressive breakfast that would safely see you through to your next meal in the evening. If my memory serves me right; he was called Bill McDonald and was a very popular B&B establishment for enthusiasts at the time. The only problem was when Bill attended an event on a Saturday evening at his local Rugby Union club, which I suspect involved the odd drink or two. This would usually result with him not being in the best of shape on a Sunday morning, especially to prepare a huge fried breakfast. Fortunately, he always did and you would then struggle to walk down the road to Haymarket station as you had just experienced one of Bill's monster Full English breakfasts. These were happy times and continued until the end of the Type 2 diesels workings in Scotland.

My first Scottish Class 37 of the trip, 37188 at Dumbarton
08.40 Fort William to Glasgow Queen Street - 23rd September 1985

One of the main reasons for being in Scotland a Type 2, Class 26: 26028
Prior to working the 16.10 portion to Liverpool Lime Street as far as Carstairs
Edinburgh Waverley station on the 27th September 1985

1985 became a fairly important year for me, as I managed to leave Shell and start a new role as The User Support Manager at the former Manchester Polytechnic during August 1985. This would be my final job, as I had decided to settle down and use my previous work experience to develop an institutional wide support network for the use of Information Technology across all Faculties and support functions.

The Polytechnic gained University status during 1992 along with most other Polytechnics across Britain and changed its name to The Manchester Metropolitan University (MMU). I would remain at MMU until I took early retirement just prior to my 59th birthday in 2010 and a good point to conclude the writing of my first book. Hopefully the book will give both my daughters and Grandchildren an insight into my life as a youngster through to the time when I finally hung up my boots and started life in retirement.

I've certainly enjoyed an interesting and varied life and hope I've got a few more years to possibly write a follow up to this book. Who knows?

Daughters - Lisa and Stephanie during Christmas 2006

St Georges C of E Junior School Circa 1958-59
With myself on the top row, second from the left.

Printed in Great Britain
by Amazon